A Native American
T H E O L O G Y

A Native American
THEOLOGY

Clara Sue Kidwell
Homer Noley
George E. "Tink" Tinker

ORBIS BOOKS

Maryknoll, New York 10545

Third printing, September 2003

The Catholic Foreign Mission Society of America (Maryknoll) recruits and trains people for overseas missionary service. Through Orbis Books, Maryknoll aims to foster the international dialogue that is essential to mission. The books published, however, reflect the opinions of their authors and are not meant to represent the official position of the society.

To obtain more information about Maryknoll and Orbis Books, please visit our website at www.maryknoll.org.

Library of Congress Cataloging-in-Publication Data

Kidwell, Clara Sue.
    A Native American theology / Clara Sue Kidwell, Homer Noley, George E. "Tink" Tinker.
      p. cm.
    Includes index.
    ISBN 1-57075-361-X (pbk.)
      1. Indians of North America—Religion. 2. Indian mythology—North America. 3. Christianity and culture—North America. 4. Christianity and other religions—North America. I. Noley, Homer, 1932- II. Tinker, George E. III. Title.

E98.R3 K53 2001
230'.089'97--dc21

00-065267

CONTENTS

PREFACE

All too often, non-Natives unconsciously homogenize Native Americans, leveling differences among them. They want to know what Indians—all Indians—think or believe about a given matter. The answer does not lie here. As we try to make clear throughout this book, there cannot be a single Native American theology. The histories and experiences of the indigenous peoples of this continent are too diverse to be accounted for in any such enterprise. The many voices of Native America cannot be contained in one effort. Rather, we present *a* Native American theology, not *the* Native American theology. We as authors come from different tribal traditions and different kinds of academic institutions and orientations, and we cannot presume to speak for all Native people.

In writing this book, we have followed the more or less traditional format of a Christian systematic theology. We did so in order to make the book most accessible to a non-Native audience. We acknowledge, however, that this strategy is problematic. A systematics beginning with creation and ending with eschatology and ultimate salvation, with interim stops at deity, theological anthropology, Christology, and the like, does not neatly fit the experiences and needs of Native Americans. We have therefore included two categories more in keeping with Native worldviews—land and trickster. There are other categories specific to various tribes that we cannot include.

Our intent is to challenge the traditional categories of Christian theology with a new understanding of Native views and to bring new insights to an understanding of Native theology, in its broadest sense. We must understand the experiences of Native communities with Christianity in both a historical sense and in terms of contemporary experience.

This is not to say that there are not commonalties of experience and worldview that many Natives share. We have tried to reflect these, as best we can, but even so, many Native people will disagree with what we have to say. There is an old saying in Indian Country that if you put six Indians in a room, you'll have seven opinions represented. We, in fact, welcome such disagreement. Not even the authors of this book have agreed about everything contained herein. We see this project as part of on-going dialogues that are happening in Indian communities—a beginning of conversation about the role of Christianity in Native life rather than a final pronouncement from on high—what Gerald Vizenor would call a "last lecture" or a "terminal creed."

Our communities have always arrived at an approximation of truth and right action through honest sharing, discussion, and consensus. This is our sharing. We believe that any Native American theology must, as far as possible, be inclusive of all Natives (traditional, Christian, neo-traditional, syncretic). We hope that this book will further the discussion and that those who disagree with us will challenge us by setting down their own thoughts and thus continuing the dialogue. Critique is not dismissal. We hope that those for whom we wrote this book will not dismiss us but will instead engage us. We know our knowledge is far from perfect and that we all have much to learn from each other.

The idea for this book grew out of such a dialogue carried on in meetings of the Native American Theological Forum, held annually since 1993 by the National United Methodist Native American Center, located at the Claremont School of Theology in California. The Forum brings together both traditional and Christian Indians. Some of the chapters in this book originated in various presentations at this Forum. The importance of presenting the ideas in the Forum to a broader audience inspired one of us (Homer Noley) to seek support from the United Methodist Church to bring together the authors of the book for this joint project.

The project brought the authors together in a dialogue of their own. Though this was a fully collaborative effort, each of the three authors took primary drafting responsibility for individual chapters. Drafts of the sections circulated freely among the writing team and were subjected to intense discussion and argument. An advisory committee of Native scholars and religious practitioners was brought together on two occasions for discussion and review of the project. The advisory committee is an essential part of our community, to whom we recognize our responsibility. They provided the invaluable feedback that helped assure that we were addressing issues that Native communities recognize and consider to be important.

Major editing of the manuscript to ensure consistency of style and tone was undertaken by Clara Sue Kidwell, with the editorial assistance of Heindrick Pieterse, publications manager for the United Methodist Church.

Some discussion of terminology is necessary. What to call the indigenous peoples of North America has, in recent years, become a source of considerable confusion and discussion. The collective terms "American Indian" and "Native American" are both, of course, constructs, and each is a problem for its own reasons. Nonetheless, we have employed these terms, along with "Native," more or less interchangeably. Where possible and appropriate we have referred to specific tribal/national traditions and groups. For White Americans, we have used the term "Amer-European," recovered from the writings of Osage author John Joseph Mathews, rather than the more familiar "Euro-American."

There are a number of people who must be thanked. Jace Weaver contributed immeasurably to the conceptualization of the project and to the initial drafting of various sections of the text. We thank those who participated in sessions of the advisory committee: Brad Drowning Bear, Harry Long, Paul Ojibway, Andrea Smith, Inés Talamantez, and Robert Warrior. Thanks to Sharon Hels and Heindrick Pieterse for their editorial help. Funding for research and writing was generously made available by the General Board of Higher Education and Ministry of The United Methodist Church and its director of the Division of Ordained Ministry, Kil Sang Yoon. Thanks as well to the National United Methodist Native American Center and its current executive director, Cynthia Abrams, for their continuing participation and support throughout the project. Finally, thanks to Orbis Books and its editor-in-chief, Robert Ellsberg, for both their willingness to publish this work and their great patience in waiting for its delivery.

And now, let the discussion begin.

Clara Sue Kidwell
Homer Noley
George Tinker

INTRODUCTION

Ts'its'tsi'nako, Thought Woman,
Is sitting in her room
And whatever she thinks about appears.
                                        Leslie Marmon Silko[1]

This American Indian theology will begin with a clear memory of how we got where we are today and a communal act of re-visioning who we are. It will mean taking our cultures, their values and traditions, seriously in order to re-imagine our future. We remember the past in order to dream or imagine the future into existence. One key starting point in this process of remembering and dreaming is that it must be clearly identified as an Indian process. We cannot allow someone else to remember or dream on our behalf.

Our Purpose

Our purpose in this volume is to create a dialogue in which Indian people can speak as equals to Christians, and where we can encourage a creative, new, visioning process for Native people where they can recognize the uniqueness of their practices with regard to Christianity. We envision renewed health for Indian cultures and each Indian national community.

This vision, however, must be built on Indian cultures, values and religious traditions, even as it responds to the devastating history of colonialism. We will present an analysis of

American Indian cultures and religious traditions—in the broadest and most pervasive sense. Since Christian theological traditions have become so pervasive in Indian communities, our theology will use many of these categories as comparative starting places, even as we challenge them and propose Indian theological categories that might serve us far better.

Christianity consistently expresses concern for freedom ("You are free in Christ Jesus" Gal 5:1.), yet it is never quite clear in the context of Indian Christianity how far that notion of freedom extends. How free are Indians to interpret Christianity for themselves (whether biblical text or Christian doctrine)? Can we assert a particularly Indian hermeneutic? We do so in Chapter One.

Our questions of interpretation move beyond the traditional logical limits of Christian interpretation. This leap of understanding means, at the least, that Indian Christians will no longer merely accede to being consumers of Amer-European theological ideas. We seize responsibility for our own spiritual well-being and generate our own interpretive theologies—whether Christian or traditional.

The Christian claim to exclusive access to spiritual truth is less and less tenable in today's world. With the expansion of communication and economic forces of globalization, it is increasingly common for business ventures, intellectual conferences, youth meetings, and the like to be multi-cultural and inter-religious events. Yet American Indian communities are still feeling the effects of missionary activities which proclaim Indian inadequacy and Christian superiority. Moreover, a major segment of American Christianity still proclaims a peculiar and defining authority for its own sacred text. Yet this claim makes a necessary two-step leap of faith. First, it must proclaim an a priori importance and superiority for written texts. Second, it must proclaim a similar a priori importance and authority for its own "sacred text," the Hebrew Bible and the Greek Testament.

Our attempt at writing an American Indian theology must struggle with other forms of "sacred text." Indian cultures, without written languages, value the spoken word (just as the early Christian community did), implying that for Indian peoples a sacred text would be invested in the oral traditions of a community. Thus the notion of a sacred text must be expanded to include both literary and non-literary works. Moreover, this means that the exclusive privileging of the Christian Bible (Hebrew Bible and Greek Testament) must also give way to a recognition of the numerous ways in which the Sacred Mystery/Sacred Other/God has chosen to communicate with the Sacred's children in different parts of the world. The special privileging of the Jesus story must be weighed against the stories of Native people. Our chapter on Christology addresses this issue.

That weighing is especially important in light of the popularizing of Indian culture in contemporary society, and the search for enlightenment and community by non-Indians. Not every articulate utterance by an Indian person, even when they claim "traditional" status, is necessarily an authoritative part of that tradition. The problem is especially acute when Indian figures, popular or well known in the White world, are summoned up to give evidence for the "tradition."

Control of sacred knowledge is essential to the integrity of native religions. Non-Indians have seized on this idea of esoteric knowledge to sell workshops and sweat lodges to people seeking spiritual enlightenment. Articulate political leaders are sometimes cited as sources of traditional knowledge, but they are generally not the custodians of tradition. Sacred knowledge resides in the elders who have heard the stories of previous generations.

We hope to provide useful insight into general categories of Indian existence and epistemology, including traditional Christian categories of Deity, Christology, Sin, and Eschatology. We must distinguish the values and practices of Indian cultures from the values and practices of Amer-European culture. We hope to suggest ways that Indian Christians might take responsibility for interpreting the gospel for Indian peoples in the context of Indian cultures and sets of values.

Our interpretation of both Christian and American Indian traditions also challenges Indian people to examine their beliefs. Some may reaffirm their faith. Others may decide to abandon churches in order to maintain their national ceremonial traditions in lieu of participation even in Indian Christianity. Others may decide to work towards some common ground of understanding between their Indian traditional identity and their identity as faithful Indian Christians. They may attempt some syncretic merging of Christianity, in terms of their own cultural interpretation of the gospel and their national religious traditions.

This book is intended for both students of theology undergoing formal training and Indian readers who have some cultural competency in Native communities. Throughout the writing of this text, we have sought advice and input from respected Indian elders. Furthermore, as Indian authors we are writing out of our own experience of the Indian world. American Indians and other indigenous peoples have a long-standing confidence that our cultures have much to teach Europeans and North Americans about the world and human relationships in the world. We are confident in the spiritual foundations of Indian cultural values, confident that those foundations can become a source of healing and reconciliation for all Creation. Thus, we expect that non-Indian readers of this volume will find much of value here that could transform the ways Amer-European people think and act theologically.

Indian Theology and the Dream of Freedom

An attempt to explicate an American Indian theology is an assertion of tribal sovereignty, the doctrine that Indian nations are sovereign entities with powers of self-government deriving from their original occupation of their lands before European contact. The assertion challenges the effects of European colonization and the role that Christianity played as a weapon used against Indian cultures. Tribal sovereignty is a political statement, and it is inextricably linked with the concept of cultural integrity. In the United States today, Indian people must be able to demonstrate the ways in which their cultural practices, ways of viewing the world, and sense of group identity set them apart as distinctive peoples from the rest of American society. Although they may participate freely in the broader society, they still have status as members of sovereign nations with powers based not only in legal principles but in an understanding of tribal culture.

Our statement of theology and cultural integrity challenges the usual history of attempts by colonial powers, the United States government, Christian missionaries, and European settlers to either eradicate or assimilate American Indians. Hunger for free land; the promise of material wealth; fear of the unknown; the image of the Indian as agent of the Devil; the need for settlers to identify themselves as righteous—all of these factors contributed to the destruction of Indian people and to the breakdown of Indian communities.

It is true that the very social fabric that once held Indian communities together has been torn apart by the continuing events of the European invasion. Whether local Indian communities are traditional reservation-based communities or new urban communities, they exhibit dramatic levels of poverty and disease. Statistics repeatedly report American Indian people in the worst position of any ethnic community in North America: the highest rates of unemployment, alcoholism, teen-age suicides, school drop-outs, and the lowest rates of longevity, education attained, per capita income, etc.[2]

If our theology is to be a part of a people's life-giving, life-sustaining social structure, and if it is to serve the ends of tribal sovereignty, it must speak not only out of past Native American experiences and cultures, but it must also speak to the contemporary reality of Native American existence. It must begin the process of imagining a new and healthy future that can provide Indian people with a sense of hope.

Knowing Our History

William Apess, a Pequot and a Methodist clergyman, in 1833 challenged criticisms of Indian peoples by white Christians: "Have you the folly to think that the white man, being one in fifteen or sixteen, are the only beloved images of God? Can you charge the Indians with robbing a nation almost of their whole continent and murdering their women and children and then depriving the remainder of their lawful rights, that nature and God require them to have?"[3] We offer a similar challenge to contemporary Christianity. Native peoples are the recipients of the revelation of God. The right to live in peace and safety with God's gift of resources belongs to Native people as well as to other peoples.

Any statement of Native theology must be based in a historical understanding of the experiences of Native people and Christian missionaries. Converting the native people of North America to Christianity was a major objective of European colonizers. As Indians were drawn into the fur and deerskin trade with Europeans, they were drawn into the emerging capitalist economy of Europe. The Protestant ethic of hard work, thrift, and industry complemented the secular motives of traders and exploitative government agents.

In Indian cultures, religious experiences in dreams, visions, or initiation create a very personal relationship between the individual and the spiritual world that manifests itself in the physical world. This understanding gives individuals a sense of control over their own lives. They can call upon spirits for their cooperation and thus achieve a sense of control over the natural world around them. This sense of personal empowerment contrasts sharply with the Christian sense of total human dependence upon the will of a supremely powerful God. It is easy to see why Indian people may not be willing to accept a Christian God who asks them to lay aside their personal powers in favor of an abstract and distant concept of salvation.

English and French Jesuits interpreted this sense of personal relationship with deity as the Catholic sin of Pride, a feeling that the individual is equal with God. They spoke of "reducing" the Indians, bringing them down from their sense of equality and making them conform to Christian values of submission to the laws of God.[4] John Eliot, the Puritan minister who converted members of several tribes around Massachusetts Bay to

Christianity, segregated his converts in communities where they were designated as "Praying Indians" and subjected to a set of rules that Eliot promulgated in 1646. It forbade, among other things, "pow-wowing" and picking lice.[5] The ultimate effect of Christian mission activity was to remove the Indian person from relationship to the tribal group in order to associate him or her with the artificial community of Christ.[6]

With Christianity, however, also came epidemic diseases, which Puritan divines viewed as acts of God. In 1634 John Winthrop, seeing the decimation of the Massachusetts Bay Indians by a smallpox epidemic, was moved to declare that the Indians ". . . are neere all dead of the small Poxe, so as the Lord hathe cleared our title to what we possess. . . ."[7] Warfare reduced Indian populations, in some cases dramatically, as with the destruction of over 300 Pequot men, women, and children at Mystic, Connecticut, during the Pequot "War" of 1636-37.

The results of disease and conflict were the disruption and displacement of Indian community life. When traditional Indian curing ceremonies failed to stem the spread of smallpox, measles, cholera, and other epidemics, traditional belief in the powers of deities, plants, animals, and other natural forces began to fail. When heavy loss of population made it impossible for survivors to carry on traditional systems of obligations, responsibility, and mutual support, social systems crumbled. Under these pressures, Christianity became a panacea, conversion a way to physical survival as much as spiritual salvation. James Axtell demonstrates how Indian groups whose lives were most disrupted by disease and alcohol and whose communities were surrounded by white settlers were most likely to accept Christianity. "Praying towns," however, were still distinctly Indian enclaves.[8]

Religious conversion became a policy tool of the United States government in the early nineteenth century in the Civilization Act (1819), which provided $10,000 to support the work of "benevolent institutions" which would teach Indians to read, write, farm, and generally live like their white neighbors.[9] The benevolent institutions were primarily missionary organizations whose objective was to convert Indians to Christianity but whose schools met the aims of the Civilization Act. The challenge to missionaries among American Indian tribes in the early nineteenth century was to find the appropriate mechanism for conversion. Should they first preach the word of God, assuming that it had efficacy in and of itself, or should they educate Indian people to read and write and translate the Gospel into Indian languages so that it would be read and understood by potential converts? In either case, the purpose was not only to convert Indians to Christianity but to imbue them with the basic attributes of white American society—submission to the authority of God, thrift, and hard work.

Indians and Christians

The patterns of Indian response to Christianity have been extraordinarily variable over time. We address some of these patterns in Chapter Five. Some people have accepted Christianity as part of the process of assimilation into American society. Some may have voluntarily converted to gain what they saw as the advantages of contact with white society; others, especially children, received Christianity through a process not always of their own choosing. Through acculturation, abetted primarily by boarding schools which took young people out of their own cultural milieux to expose them fully to Christian values, Indian students' native value systems were replaced by the teachings of missionaries. Presbyterian mission schools in the Choctaw and Cherokee nations in the early 1800's impressed upon students their sinfulness and inspired that anxiety for the fate of their souls that was a primary sign of conversion.

If Christian missionaries mounted deliberate attacks on Indian cultures, some Indians were nevertheless able to turn religious experience to the revitalization of their own communities and to bring a renewed interest in cultural traditions to their people. Handsome Lake, a Seneca man, had a series of visions from 1799 to 1801 in which he saw Christ, George

Washington, and a series of scenes of punishment for various wrongdoings. He preached a new native gospel, the Gaiwiio, in which he urged his people to revive traditional ceremonial practices of feasting and dreaming to communicate with the spirits, although his doctrine also denounced certain traditional practices of witchcraft and promoted the nuclear family over the traditional extended matrilineages. Handsome Lake's visions gave new hope to a demoralized nation.[10] In other cases, groups adopted certain symbols and doctrines from Christianity and thus accommodated certain new understandings of religious experience. A number of Pueblo groups in the Southwest adopted Catholic saints and rituals as part of their religious ceremonies. Although some have considered themselves Catholics, their beliefs have not been accepted by the Catholic Church; and conversely, although the Catholic Church considered some as true converts, they did not consider themselves so.[11]

The Catholic Church has asserted domination over Indian belief systems through the doctrine of inculturation, which asserts that God is central to all cultural experiences because culture is based in experiences of nature, and God is the creator of nature. "Inculturation is an ongoing reciprocal process between faith and culture. It is a way of looking at the customs, rites, and rituals of people to discover in them the active and saving presence of God. Through inculturation the Church affirms what is good in a culture; purifies what is false and evil; strengthens what is weak; educates what is ignorant."

In the model of inculturation, conversion entails a modification of cultural experience rather than a complete denial of it. Some cultural practices can be considered as forms of Christianity, while others may be eradicated.[12] The assertion that Indian religions are simply different cultural forms of Christianity is an example of that claim to universality and exclusivity that has characterized Christian attempts to dominate and subduc Indians throughout history.

In contemporary American society, there are many Native people who profess strong belief in and allegiance to Christian churches of various denominations. Some totally reject traditional Indian cultural beliefs, and some integrate Christianity and traditional practices. The degree to which Christianity represents a rejection of Native traditions is a function of history. It is also a function of changing models of what constitutes culture. It is, above all, a recognition of the fact that culture is a very fluid concept, that adaptation and change are part of the human historical experience, and that belief is a very personal thing.

The Question of Conversion

Can one be Christian and Indian simultaneously in contemporary society? This is the ultimate question in the relationship between contemporary Native people and organized Christian churches. Many Indian people, for a great variety of reasons, have found it useful, or practical, or necessary, to convert to Christianity. Early on in the missionizing enterprise, many converted out of desperation. Death and illness left communities severely weakened—sometimes with a population reduced by more than ninety percent. In the face of the overwhelming power of the advancing White world, conversion was an attempt to stave off continuing disaster and to access for themselves the perceived power of Whites.

Today, many of us are of mixed ancestry, Indian and non-Indian, and have been brought into Christianity through Amer-European Christian parentage. Some full bloods made the conversion simply because they could see the privileged status of mixed-bloods in comparison to themselves. Conversion, then, was an attempt to mimic the mixed-blood experience and gain some of the advantage that White Amer-Europeans typically bestowed on mixed-bloods.

For some, the new religious connection became a syncretic melding of traditional and Christian beliefs. The Yaqui communities of the Southwest provide prime examples of this syncretic melding: Christian concepts of good and evil are enacted in an annual ceremony at Easter in which a battle takes place between the followers of Jesus and those of the Devil.[13]

For others, the conversion was much more shallow—merely an outward appearance or surface structure. In many of these contexts, the traditional spiritual structures of the ancients actually continue to live as sort of a parallel universe to the missionary religion. The outward commitment to the missionary religion allows for a layer of protection for the traditional cultural values and the ceremonial forms that accompany those values.

Indian Christians must balance their cultural values and Christian doctrines. This balancing act has been necessary throughout history. Where Christianity creates a community that shares a belief in religious dogma and responsibility to obey God, Native communities stress obligations to kinfolk. Conflicting loyalties can have disastrous consequences, as they did at the Hopi village of Awatovi in 1700. There, men from other villages attacked and killed Christian converts who no longer carried out Hopi ceremonial obligations.[14] Although this is an extreme example, Indian Christians in conservative Indian communities can still face significant social pressures from relatives and friends.

Religion and Culture

We will argue that there are some fundamental distinctions that set American Indian cultures and religious traditions (in all of their diversity) quite apart from European and Amer-European cultures and religion. These distinctions have to do with basic world-view and philosophical orientations as well as with differences in categorization. They include categories such as religion and worship; the nature of deity; the relationship between humans and other parts of the created order; and differences in valuing space or time, community and the individual.

The earliest English colonizers of North America attempted to justify their invasion of Indian lands by describing the aboriginal owners of these lands as uncivilized. One of the tests of civilization applied by the English was whether the indigenous inhabitants had a religion. Desirous of Indian land and not seeing a church steeple anywhere in sight, they proclaimed that Indian people had no religion and thus could not be considered civilized.

In their cultural myopia, these English forebears of modern Americans were both right and wrong. Those indigenous communities had intensely spiritual lives filled with countless daily ceremonial acts (personal and communal) and regular seasonal ceremonies of whole communities. But they had no religion. Typically, elders in almost any Indian community today, especially those who carry ceremonial responsibilities, will deny that their community ever had a religion. Rather, they will argue, their whole cultural and social structure was and still is infused with a spirituality that cannot be separated from the rest of the community's life at any point. The Green Corn Ceremony, the Snake Dance, kachinas, the Sun Dance, sweat-lodge ceremonies, and the sacred pipe are not specifically religious constructs of various tribes, but rather represent specific ceremonial aspects of a world that includes countless ceremonies in any given tribal context, ceremonies performed by whole communities, clans, families, or individuals on a daily, periodic, seasonal, or occasional basis. Contemporary Indian ceremonial practices range from sings or chants on the Navajo reservation to stomp dances at Creek grounds in Oklahoma to Sun Dances on reservations in the Northern plains. Such ceremonials all have the aspect of human participation in renewing the processes of the world.

Whereas outsiders may identify a single ritual as the religion of a particular people, the people themselves will likely see that ceremony as merely an extension of their day-to-day existence, all parts of which are experienced within ceremonial parameters and should be seen as "religious."[15] Thus, this theology treats the whole of Indian life as a religious phenomenon and does not try to separate out part of that existence in order to fit it into the Amer-European category of religion.

Space, Time, and Place

Christianity portends teleology. Time, or history, is going someplace. There is a goal for human existence, whether that goal is measured in terms of moral progress, Christian sanctification, dialectical materialism, manifest destiny, or capitalist globalization. Likewise, individuals are headed someplace, in historical time, whether in career development, faith development, moral development, or ultimate salvation. The teleological sense of time in the Christian sense is the working out of God's plan on earth, and it places human beings in a special status. The object of God's will is ultimate salvation for human beings.

American Indian traditions are spatially based rather than temporally based. Indian people lived their lives in accordance with the cycles of nature. While western scientists see space and time as two distinct dimensions of reality, Indian cultures value their association with their homelands and often patterned the organization of their villages and their ceremonies to the spatial movements of the sun and stars in the world above. Where Christianity is oriented to an ultimate end in heaven, Native time is oriented to the repetition of events. Spatial categories are determinative for an American Indian reality; Amer-Europeans value time. This dichotomy is obviously not absolute. Indian communities understand the progress of events through time, and Christian ceremonies echo seasonal cycles. The importance of cycles in nature is paramount in Indian communities.

The temporal orientation of contemporary society has fueled the industrial revolution and continues to fuel modern economic systems (capitalist or Marxist). Without a firm sense of the temporal and technology to match—e.g., production schedules, time clocks for commodifying labor; calendars, personal wrist watches; and computers programmed to handle changes from daylight to standard time—the entire military-industrial infrastructure of the United States would collapse.

In the cyclical patterns of time in Indian communities, human beings are simply part of the ongoing process of repetition of events in the environment—hunting seasons, agricultural cycles. What is important is that these events reoccur on a regular basis. The object of much of the ceremonialism in subsistence-based Indian cultures was to assure that these cycles did indeed repeat themselves.

The sense of the immanent power of deity is apparent in all the operations of the environment that involve movement and change. Because people express in prayer their hope that corn will grow or animals will return to the hunting ground, their words have a creative power in the universe. The expenditure of human energy is essential to the operation of deity in the world.

Because power is manifest in all the things of the world, the sacred may appear at any time. People are constantly reminded of the presence of deity as they pass by certain rock formations, or rivers, or groves of trees. Thus space, rather than time, becomes the evidence of God's presence in the world in an immediate manner. Spatiality and the notion of interrelatedness lend themselves to a categorical difference between these indigenous cultures and the West. Unlike nomadic European settlers whose impulse to explore drove men across the Atlantic in their search for wealth, American Indian traditions tell of their origins in specific places, of their emergence from worlds below or descent from the sky above to where they are now, or of their migrations, led by spiritual guides, to homelands that were designated for them. In Chapter Eight we address this sense of a spiritual association with land, the marking of boundaries and renewal of the earth through ceremonies, and the concept of Earth as mother and nurturer.

Indian communities have an attachment both historically and presently to particular lands, and our cultural identity is heavily invested in that attachment. It helps to define the limits of our ceremonial life, to give a foundation to our traditional stories and myths, to secure a sense of balance and harmony in community identity. Throughout our colonial history, land has been the source of conflict. Loss of land and forcible migrations led to destruction of Indian communities and tremendous loss of life. Land was the basis of the treaties made between Indian tribes and the United States government. Land is today the basis upon which tribal sovereignty rests, the rights of Indian people to live upon, to use, and to govern in a political sense the members of the tribe who live on the land and those whose tribal membership gives them an association with it.

The Value of Community

American Indian indigenous cultures are communitarian/ communitist by nature. The nature of tribal societies is defined by the social structures of kinship rather than by the importance of the individual. Who one's family is defines one's sense of self. The Lakota *tiospaye* is the extended family unit upon whose honor and reputation the behavior of the young warrior or Sun Dancer reflects. The *owachira* is the extended matrilineage which selects the men who serve as sachems in the Grand League of the Iroquois. Clan affiliations determine who may and who may not marry among the Navajo.

Kin relationships structure the rights, obligations, and responsibilities of individuals toward the group. In Indian communities, people are valued not for what they achieve for themselves but for what they contribute to the stability and continuity of the group. At the same time, tribal societies recognize the uniqueness and personal identity of individuals. These sources of individual identity and power are found in the relationship between the individual and the spiritual world. The elements of personality are both the sense of dependency upon the spiritual world for all power, and the sense of personal ability once a relationship has been established with those spiritual forces to control or influence power.

The form and phenomena of power come to the individual as esoteric knowledge. The mystical experience of personal contact with the spiritual world is both a profoundly emotional one and one in which specific information is imparted to the recipient. That information can then be said to inform individual behavior by providing a basis for action. It is the knowledge that is the essence of power. Knowledge of the spirit world can be gained in the active vision quest practiced by men in Plains tribes, in dreams; in initiation rites, as among the Pueblo peoples of the southwest; and for women, during their seclusion during their menstrual cycles. This spiritual experience informs personal behavior, and the individual talents or aptitudes of men and women are signs of it.

Ceremonies become ways in which groups of people come together not only to communicate with deities but to valorize the roles that individuals play within the group. The young women who attend Sun Dancers must be virgins, and their very participation in the society is an acknowledgment of their status as chaste and potentially marriageable young women. In an Indian community, personal behavior is under constant scrutiny for its appropriateness and, in traditional societies, affirmation that the individual stands in proper relationship to all other members of the community and to the spirit world.

Gender

Native societies valued women as mothers of future generations and repositories of tribal wisdom. The roles of men and women were complementary rather than hierarchic as in the Christian ideal of the power of men.[16] Neither were they patriarchal in the oppressive sense that we have come to identify male privilege in the modern world. Many traditional Indian cultures were and are matriarchal in that lineage and residence are determined through female lines. Still today in many Iroquoian tribes in the United States and Canada, each male chief is appointed to this responsibility by his clan mother. He serves at her pleasure, and no decision can be made in council without final ratification of the clan mothers. In a great many other tribes, the home itself was characteristically owned by the women, an intentional social device for balancing gender power relationships within the society. Political decision-making in aboriginal North America was predicated on a domestic base, that is, on the smallest social unit of the female-controlled home, rather than hierarchically from some ruling council, from the top down[17]

It is important in this regard that American Indian experiences of "god" included almost invariably a bi-gender, reciprocal duality of male and female: e.g., Earth and Sky, Grandmother and Grandfather, Above and Below, Day and Night. Colonization of language, however, has meant that even traditional speakers when speaking in the colonial language (English) will customarily reference the bi-gender Wakonda with the male pronouns, "he," "his," and "him," although they would never do this in their native language. Yet when we pray in the traditional way, we still call upon that bi-gender duality of male and female, represented by Sky and Earth, the two great fructifying powers of the Creator.

The power of women is symbolized in the reciprocal duality of deity, and it is certainly reinforced in the traditions of Native people.[18] The specific manifestation of deity as creator is quite often female, particularly in the Southwest. For the Hopi, Pueblos, and Navajos, for instance, a female power functions as creator, the shaper of human life: Spider Woman, Thought Woman, Changing Woman. If women are respected throughout the Indian world as "life givers," even as somehow superior to men because of their ability to bring new life into the community, it is only natural that this respect is a reflection of female spiritual power in the larger creational process.

Thus, in spite of the concerted efforts of missionaries and U.S. government agencies to teach Indian peoples the superior worth of men, Indian communities continue to remember things about the balancing of genders and even a certain privileging of women. While Indian men may fall too easily into Christian patterns of male hierarchy, Indian women constantly stand as strong reminders of a different way of being in each of our communities. And, ultimately, Indian men know the truth of the old Indian aphorism that our nations will never die until the hearts of our women lie on the ground.

Ethical Values and the Concept of Sin

The value systems of tribal societies are determined not by dogmatic rules but by the expectations of the community. Ethics asks the question, What is good? The answer in Indian communities lies in two dimensions. For the individual, good is long life, good health, and happiness. It is achieved by remaining in proper relationship to all people, all beings in the physical world, and the spirits. The Navajo speak of *hózhó*, a term generally glossed as "beauty," but which Gary Witherspoon defines as "the ideal environment of beauty, harmony, and happiness."[19] The ideal of harmony entails fulfilling one's responsibilities to the community. Spirituality is a way of gaining access to power that can then be used for the good of the community. It defines the roles that people play in relation to other people. Appropriate behavior is the basis for ethical behavior.

The mechanisms for social control in Indian societies are based in personal interactions rather than abstract rules. Teasing and ridicule are common ways of letting people know that they are not doing the right thing. Sacred clowns and heyokas in Pueblo and Plains ceremonies represent the disorder in the universe that is contrary to but which also reinforces ideas of harmony and balance, and their actions remind people of the proper way of doing things. Trickster figures in oral traditions demonstrate both the creative power of deity but also how immoderate and deceitful behavior always leads to misfortune. The Cibecue Apache remind people of their inappropriate behavior by telling stories of similar events in which the individual met some untoward fate at some place in the physical environment. Whenever the persons who committed the offense pass that place, they are reminded of their behavior.[20]

The Christian concepts of original sin and salvation through Christ are antithetical to Indian concepts of personal power based on dreams, visions, and initiation into esoteric knowledge of deity. Indian languages did not have words for these concepts of sin and salvation. The Choctaw words glossed as sin by Cyrus Byington, a Presbyterian missionary in the 1820's, meant to make a mistake or to be lost in the wilderness. The Choctaw speaker, hearing Byington preach about sin in 1823, would understand sin either as a form of mistake or as losing one's way in the woods. Such meanings, by extension, convey some aspects of sin in Christianity but certainly do not connote either the depths of human depravity that sin represented in the strongly Calvinist tradition of Protestantism or the stain of original sin in Catholicism.

From the Indian point of view, sin can be defined as a failure to live up to one's responsibility, sometimes deliberately but more likely as a result of impulsive or unthinking behavior, a mistake. Salvation can be defined as the ability to return to a state of communitas. The Cherokee had certain towns that were sacred sites where people could seek sanctuary when they had transgressed social norms. The Green Corn Ceremony was a time of forgiveness that restored all people to proper relationships.

In contemporary society, politicians call for the dissolution of tribal sovereignty and Indian land bases. Their arguments are generally based on the idea that Indians receive special privileges such as tax advantages and immunity from American legal processes. Although Indian communities are often mired in poverty, their special status vis-à-vis the United States government is the result of a long historical process of interaction between sovereign nations and the cession of Indian land in exchange for services and a special relationship with the government. To deny this relationship would be the final injustice to Indian people. The land that is the basis for Indian religious beliefs translates in contemporary American society into both cultural and political identity for Indian people.

Our attempt to explicate a Native American theology is ultimately rooted in a holistic sense of Native cultures. Although we use Christian theological categories of inquiry, the reality is that time, space, land, kin, community, and deity are inextricably linked. Knowledge of the sacred is a matter both of individual insight and shared understanding. We must respect the power of esoteric knowledge which cannot be shared while seeking to make accessible an understanding of Native spiritual beliefs. The following chapters suggest the links among categories that Christian theology has traditionally separated.

Chapter 1

HERMENEUTICS

Origin of Belief

*T*he story is told of a construction company which con-
tracted to build a bridge across a major river. The
company decided to start building the bridge from both
sides of the river. The engineers calculated that the two sections of the bridge, starting from each side of the river,
would meet in the exact center of the river where the bridge
would be completed by joining the two sections. When the
day finally came that the two sections were to be joined, it
was discovered that there had been a slight miscalculation
by one or the other side and the beams of the two sections did
not arrive at the middle of the river at the same place. At
least one half of the project had to be abandoned.

told by Homer Noley

Any written text is subject to interpretation, and interpretation is essential as a bridge of understanding between different
traditions. The Bible was written in particular times and places
by individuals who were products of their own cultural backgrounds. American Indian traditions similarly come from par-

ticular times and cultures. The issue of interpretation is crucial to an examination of the roots of belief and understanding of any religious tradition.

The term "hermeneutics" has roots in Greek mythology. Hermes in Greek mythology was the "god of boundaries, roads and commerce; of science and inventions, of eloquence, luck and cunning; and the patron of thieves and gamblers."[1] He is portrayed wearing wings on his hat and shoes, and he is described as a messenger for Zeus and other gods. Rounding out his problematic job description, he was described as "the messenger of the gods."[2] His role represents an important aspect of human communication. In every deliberation and every declaration there is an element of interpretation which has the power to impact on the conclusions. The messenger had a task which could change the course of history depending on how he interpreted the information given him at one point and how he delivered it at another point.

Differing Bases for Interpretation of the Bible

Christianity depends upon the hermeneutics of biblical scholars to shed light on the meaning of Christ's life and teachings. The Gospel that reached the native people of North America was interpreted by scholars who were products of their own cultural backgrounds in the intellectual traditions of Western Europe. Their interpretations which emerged from particular Western European experiences have, however, been adopted as standards of religious truth.

If the hermeneutical choices of previous biblical scholars have been allowed to shape the expression of Christianity, should not Indian people approach the interpretation of Scripture from their own cultural perspectives? Because Indian people may read the Bible from a different sense of culture and history, their interpretations may differ from traditional Christianity. The issue of hermeneutics as a traditional category of Christian theology is whether American Indians can interpret scripture in their own ways.

The tenets of Christianity as taught by some missionaries were not in and of themselves hostile to Native American traditions and could even be said to have been complementary in some cases. In terms of interpretation, we must ask, has the Bible supported the colonial Gospel bearers, or has violence been done to the Holy Scriptures as well?

Bible interpretation is an exercise of supreme responsibility. When one presumes to say what the Bible says, one must transcend the ever-present self-interest that may detract from the truth of the scriptures and cause one to co-opt the scripture for one's own purposes. The preliminary step in the hermeneutical process is a conscious system of checks and balances that will provide the criteria for scriptural interpretation and the means to critique our conclusions.

In the Bible we are invited to see and perceive how God worked in history among a particular people, Israel. We are to see how God has revealed Godself and God's purposes for such revelations. But the Bible also represents a period of history presented not as a historical narrative, but as a spiritual witness of that time for our time. As in the case of any history, whether it is the strict historical narrative of a people or a spiritual record of human experience, one thing about the Bible is true—it represents a period of human experience which has been arrested in time and is evidenced in written form. No matter when in time we live after that, we must construct a bridge of understanding from our time to the time of that human experience.

The hermeneutical task is perilous because we must try to make connections not only among contemporary Native communities but also between cultures distant both in time and place. Even in the days of Jesus, the hermeneutical task was perilous as the Law and the Prophets were interpreted by Christians in the wheat fields, the marketplace, and on the mountaintops.

Jesus himself may have used the hermeneutical principles of the Jewish teacher Hillel to declare his own conclusive interpretations of past teachings. The middot of Hillel contained seven rules to harmonize apparent inconsistencies and unclear passages in the Torah. Ishmale, a colleague of Hillel, developed a system of thirteen rules which included the rules of Hillel. Jewish Christian hermeneutics included Jesus' teachings and the teaching of the apostles. With the decline of Jewish Christianity at the close of the first century, gentile Christians began interpreting Jewish scriptures for the edification of the growing gentile Christian population.

Some of the principles for interpreting the scriptures used by the gentile Christians were already in use, having been applied to classical Greek literature. Certain of these, such as allegory and typology, became important in their application to Jewish and Jewish Christian scripture. During the second, third, and fourth centuries, a great deal of work was done in the search for a reasonable and spiritual approach to biblical interpretation. For this period of time the culmination of effort occurred with the formulation of the "fourfold sense of scripture" method of interpreting scripture. The four parts of this formulation are literal, allegorical, typological, and anagogical. They were intended to provide "syntheses of all the main strands of patristic hermeneutics to be handed down to the Latin Middle Ages."[3]

The basic elements of this interpretation can be expressed as:

1. accepting it for what it says;
2. seeing it for what it possibly means;
3. seeing it in terms of its meaning for one's moral life;
4. seeing it for what it means in terms of the present and future spiritual lives of people.

In contemporary times the "fourfold sense of scripture" still exists, albeit in more contemporary form. Hermeneutics must explore more appropriate standards for scriptural understanding. No longer can the hermeneutical presuppositions and practices of Northern Europe and North America be considered normative in the Christian Church. Within these cultures the perspectives of minority groups and of women enlarge, enrich, and challenge traditional understandings.[4]

Schleiermacher's approach to biblical understanding, featuring a reconstruction of the author's mental process,[5] provides a way of introducing Indian cultural values into an understanding of Christian practices. Native understanding of traditional stories within a Christian context can help us understand the interpretations of traditional practitioners. More important is to seek to understand why Native people have different interpretations of Christianity, and to realize how diverse their interpretations are.

The basic issue of hermeneutics is how any people take their own experience as a basis for understanding Christianity. As Native Americans, we must understand how contemporary Native people respond to scripture. We must examine the ways in which we see scripture. Take, for example, the story of Elijah in the Book of Kings:

> The word of God came to Elijah, "Go away from here, go east and hide by the torrent of Cherith, east of the Jordan. You can drink from the stream, and I have ordered the ravens to bring you food there." So he set out and did as God had said; he went and stayed by the torrent of Cherith, east of the Jordan. The ravens brought him bread in the morning and meat in the evening, and he quenched his thirst at the stream.
>
> But then the stream dried up for there was no rain. God said to Elijah, "Go to Zarephath in Sidonia and stay there. I have ordered a widow there to give you food." So he went to Sidon. When he reached the city gates there was a widow gathering sticks. Elijah said, "Please bring a little water in a pitcher for me to drink." She was on her way to fetch it when he called out "and also please bring me a scrap of bread to eat." "As your God lives," she replied, "I have no baked bread but only a handful of meal in a jar and a little oil in a jug. I am just gathering a stick or two to go and prepare this for myself and my son to eat and then we shall die." Elijah said to her, "Do not be afraid, go and do as you say, but first make a small piece of

bread for me, for God of Israel says this 'Jar of meal shall
not be spent—jug of oil shall not be emptied before the
day when God sends rain on the face of the earth.' " The
woman went and did as Elijah told her; and she, and he,
and her household ate for many days. The jar of meal was
not spent nor the jug of oil emptied. (1 Kings 17:3-16)

Elijah's story is interpreted as an account of the providence
of God. For American Indian communities, a sense of history
shows that the Puritans who first set foot on this land would
have starved were it not for the providence and generosity of
the coastal tribes. It is said that a prominent Puritan referred to
this story of the Bible when explaining that fact. He compared
the event to Elijah being fed by the wild beasts of the field and
made no mention of the poor widow who at least was a human
under God's command. An Indian interpretation would stress
the importance of the widow, a human being who was not of
the same religion as Elijah but whose faithfulness caused her to
respond to the God of Israel.

On another occasion, a Puritan clergyman, observing that
thousands of Native people had died from smallpox brought
by the slave trader, Captain Hunt, said, "The plague was a
wonderful preparation the Lord Jesus Christ by His providence for His people abode in the western worlds." For American Indians, the social and cultural devastation caused by epidemic diseases was sometimes seen as a punishment by the
spirits for their accepting European trade goods and customs.[6]

It is clear that these Puritan spokesmen had serious problems in assessing on one hand the tragic loss of thousands of
Native lives and on the other hand the fact that the coastal
tribes still shared food and shelter with the colonists. The issue
we address is interpretation. More to the point—who is doing
the interpretation and why is it being done that way?

Hermeneutics is the academic term designating the meth-
odology of critical interpretation. Most often associated with
biblical interpretation, it comes from a Greek root that means
simply "interpretation." In a church where absolute authority

was essential, interpretation became essential for humans seeking to understand doctrine. Hermeneutics was essential in the gentile development of Western European theology in the early church in order to establish doctrinal purity and root out heresy.

Hermeneutics is the process of interpretation that must occur when essential facts supporting objective knowledge are absent in a given circumstance, situation, or literary text. On the other hand, supporting facts may be present but a mindset fashioned by culture or special interest may block a clear view of them. Christian hermeneutics is generally the province of a small elite of individuals highly educated in the tradition they are studying. The practice and understanding of religion, however, resides in the majority of the population.[7] For hermeneutics of American Indian traditions, scholars have relied on the opinions of individuals who were holders of esoteric knowledge or leaders of ceremonies. We have seen only the elite view, not that of the everyday practitioner. The interpretation of the belief system is incomplete. Horsley says, "Until very recently the modern Western assumption is that the common people have been very conservative folk pursuing their traditional way of life and 'vegetating' in the teeth of time."[8] He shows the power of common folk to bring about religious change.

Hermeneutics is an ongoing process as new historical documents and archaeological evidence come to light. This new information continually challenges biblical interpretation. For example, the notion of a liberation movement called "Zealots" in Jesus' time is not supported by evidence gathered by research. The idea of a Zealot movement has certain usefulness for biblical scholars, but history shows that the Zealots as an organized political movement did not exist until the winter of 67-68 CE.

For modern Indian Christians, New Testament studies, "a field whose principal purpose is to interpret sacred literature," must stand in judgment for its dependence on exclusively literary means of ascertaining the nature of the origins of the Christian

church. Living oral traditions in Indian communities and archaeological findings (despite the criticism of the disruption of Indian
graves) can provide evidence for interpretation of Christian sacred literature from an enhanced understanding of Native cultures. It is essential for us to have as accurate an understanding of
native beliefs as of the social, doctrinal, and theological base of
the Christian movement.

Native Hermeneutics

It is also necessary to have self-understanding as Native people indigenous to this land. Native peoples must arrive at this
understanding by their own tests of self-determination. Government agencies, church bureaucracies, and anthropologists
have defined tribal existence by federal recognition, have quan-
tified Indian health status, economic status, social and political
status. But we must ask from a community perspective, who
are we as tribes among tribes, as Native people in the Americas, as nations within a nation? Who are we in relation to the
land? More and more, Native scholars are exerting themselves
and are breaking new ground by challenging the stream of information to which people have become accustomed. We still
have to fashion appropriate systems of defining our own
status.

Native hermeneutics must address not only interpretation
of religion, but how native communities are perceived and defined by the dominant society. It has been asserted, for example, that 80 percent of American Indian families are dysfunctional.[9] This assertion points out that the church fashions its
ministry to serve the 20 percent that is not dysfunctional.
While there is no question that the church offers many services
not usable by Native peoples because they are oriented for the
larger church, the statistic is difficult to accept. What is the
standard by which 80 percent of Native families are defined as
dysfunctional?

Even today in a time when we claim to live in a more enlightened era, Euro-Americans are still evaluating Native American lives using their own standards as the basis for judgment. Unfortunately, in far too many cases Native American leaders have bought into those standards and so judge their own people. Is a Native American family dysfunctional because it doesn't resemble a white family? A wholly traditional family under that kind of standard would, by its very nature, be dysfunctional in a white-dominated society.

Biblical hermeneutics, although burdened with the responsibility and power to determine truth, is like more mundane interpretive tasks in some ways. We pick our way through life making daily judgments about one thing or another and most times are willing to admit when bad judgments are made which in turn result in inappropriate conclusions and/or actions. If we are concerned about making bad judgments, we may seek to find criteria to guide us in the matter of interpreting things around us. Finding those criteria is itself an interpretive task. The starting point is usually to find some anchorage in our personal and community heritage and environment. Public institutions are eager to provide us with the criteria of the dominant society. Public schools emphasize American values in history and culture. Church denominations teach the principles unique to their version of Christianity. Political groups present their particular brand of prejudices. All of these entities may have some important and useful things to offer, but their negative aspects are not presented.

Seeking a Biblical Base for Interpretation

The Bible is regarded as a sacred book by Christians and has historically been under the protection of the church. No one except the authorized hermeneuts of the church could legally copy, interpret, or distribute the writings of the Bible. As the church expanded into new countries, the Bible had to be translated into new languages. Church officials feared, however, that unless a standard interpretation existed, translations would spread divergent views rather than doctrinal truth.

It appears that interpretation is a natural process by which human beings, individuals as well as communities, seek to understand their place in the universe, on their planet, and even the worth and value of the individual. In times of war, leaders must evaluate the value of human life against the ultimate effects of defeat or victory. When human life is totally devalued in terms of spiritual worth, the result is nihilism—utter worthlessness.[10] In an attempt to escape from nihilism, individuals may adopt ideological concepts as absolutes. Such assumptions are "non-sustainable" and cannot provide the ideological anchor that is needed. "They constitute zones of rebellion and remain foci of unrest." As Thielicke says, ". . . philosophies (world views) are subject to severe wear and tear. Every philosophy created by making an absolute of a relative can maintain itself for only a short time before it succumbs to the opposing forces which it has itself provoked. In this sense the history of modern thought with its succession of 'issues' is like a gigantic parade of idols. And how comical the idols that have just marched past look from behind!"[11]

It would have been easy for Native people to fall into a state of nihilism. Stripped of land, their populations decimated by disease, the American Indian population by the turn of the twentieth century had declined to about 250,000. Indian children were being taken from their homes and put into boarding schools modeled on military training establishments. Richard Pratt, an army officer who had supervised Indian prisoners of war at Fort Marion, Florida, established a school at Carlisle barracks, an abandoned military installation in Pennsylvania, in 1879. Pratt's interpretation of the Indian situation is as follows: "[T]here is a hope that they are to be permitted to become like the whites, that their declarations that they 'want to travel upon the white man's road' are at last accepted."[12]

For American Indian people, hermeneutics must extend beyond the interpretation of biblical texts. Interpretations of their cultures by government agents and Christian missionaries have led to policies that contributed to loss of language, culture, and even life. We maintain that Indian people must be able to assert their own interpretations of their cultures. These must come not only from an elite group of individuals but should represent a true community viewpoint. This viewpoint extends to interpretations of Christian doctrine from a truly Indian perspective.

Chapter 2

CREATION

Balancing the World for Seven Generations[1]

*H*eavily dressed for the two feet of snow covering the hillside, a small group of people stood quietly around what looked like a perfect, if rather large, Christmas tree. These were Christian Indians from a variety of tribes and members of an Indian congregation, who were engaging in an act of prayer, speaking prayers on behalf of the tree in preparation to cutting it and taking it with them back to their church. It could have been most any annual congregational outing to harvest a Christmas tree for their church, except that these prayers were a thorough mixture of Christian prayers and traditional Indian tribal prayers. The two Indian ministers held tobacco in their hands, ready to offer it back to the Creator, to offer it for the life of this tree, to offer it to the four directions, above and below, to offer it in order to maintain the harmony and balance of Creation even in this imminent perpetration of an act of violence. Someone wrapped a string of colorful tobacco tie offerings around the trunk. As four men sang traditional prayer songs around a drum, the people came one by one up to the tree to touch it and say their prayers, actually speaking to

*the tree, speaking consoling words of apology, gratitude,
purpose and promise. They promised the tree that its life
would be used in a positive way, a sacred way, to empower
their prayers during the times of Advent and Christmas,
and they asked its permission to take its life for this purpose.*

told by Tink Tinker

For American Indians, creation is a matter of give and take.
It is never merely a matter of explaining or knowing what happened long ago at the beginning of time but is rather a matter
of knowing our rightful place in the world and of living appropriately. Thus, this give and take is not the stuff of happen-
stance, but a life and death matter of balancing the world and
our place in it, with special attention to maintaining the world
for our children who will live seven generations from now. For
this reason, Indian religious thinking, theology, must invariably begin with creation and with understanding our place in
the world as human beings. The lessons of creation are multiple. All of creation is filled with our relatives; thus all of creation is alive. Yet we need to eat. Hence, we take whatever we
need from the plenty of creation around us; but we always give
something back in return to remind us that what we have taken
was taken at a cost to our relatives in the world around us.

Cultural value is being exposed in this gathering. There is
here an attitude toward Creation and all the createds that sets
American Indians (both Christian and traditional Indians)
apart from other Americans and from Euro-western peoples in
general. At the same time, it is rather characteristic of a great
many of the world's Indigenous Peoples and represents a set of
cultural values that perseveres even in those Indigenous communities that have been converted to Christianity. Perhaps an
outsider would describe the attitude of these Indians as one of
awe or wonderment. We American Indians think of it as neither, but would prefer to call it respect, the appropriate attitude of respect necessary to fulfill our responsibility as part of
the created whole, necessary to help maintain the harmony and

balance, the interdependence and inter-relationship of all things in our world.

Respect, then, is a key word in an American Indian cultural context, respect for a tree, for all of life, for each other, and for all of what Euro-Christians would call "Creation." Perhaps even more important is the notion that underlies the moral emphasis on respect, a notion we might call reciprocity. The prayers and the offering of tobacco are reciprocal acts of giving something back to the earth and to all of Creation in order to maintain balance even as we disrupt the balance by cutting down this tree. This chapter, which announces itself as dealing with creation, is ultimately about respect, the balancing of the world and living in reciprocity. The great variety of stories told in Indian communities about "beginnings" always have the intention of helping those communities to live in the world, not just with each other but with all of the rest of the created realm. Creation, then, is about balance and the respect and reciprocity necessary to maintain balance in the world around us.

Creation

Every Native community has various stories about its origins. Anthropologists may label these as "creation" stories. They tell of worldly and human beginnings, and variations in the stories often come from the different traditions of clans or moieties within the community, or sometimes from the different societies within the community. The word "creation" for these stories, however, presents problems for Indian people because it assumes a beginning similar to the Judeo-Christian creation story.

We can begin to get at the difference by noting some significant differences between the use of these stories in the two traditions. First, when the word is used in a Christian context, it seems to Indian peoples to connote a heavy dose of reification that is completely lacking in any Indian intellectual tradition, i.e., creation has been historically and continues to be objectified as a thing, something that is quite apart from human beings and to which humans relate from the outside. This objectification is strikingly different from the traditional Indian sense that all of the created world—including every tree and rock—is just as alive and sentient as human beings are, and the further sense that Indian peoples have that we are related to all of these sentient persons in creation.

The second thing we should note about Indian traditions is that "beginnings" stories do not function to define the beginning as a tenet of faith to be affirmed by the believer. Nor do they function to establish the ontological nature of the created world once and for all. Rather the beginnings named in the stories are merely the beginning of an on-going process. In the Christian tradition, creation happened at the beginning. God did it, and it is done. In Christian tradition, the creation story is treated as an ontological history about God (the history of God's being, the primal nature of God) that was completed in the primordial past—it happened long ago, at the beginning of time. In creation God established the world, put things in motion, and with that God's creation activity was finished. In the Christian tradition, creation stories show God's ultimate power and authority in the world.

This assertion of authority means in the Christian tradition that the world ultimately belongs to God. God gives Adam and Eve dominion over all life forms by empowering them to name all things—fishes, birds of the air, animals. God has also delegated responsibility for the earth to humans. The contemporary Christian tradition has turned from the idea of dominion to the idea of stewardship. Although this idea of stewardship may be more ecologically sensitive, it is still committed to the hierarchic privileging of humans—a concept about which we will say more.

Indian stories assume an inherent power in each part of the created whole. They show how human beings deal with the specific powers identified with different manifestations of the Sacred Other, the source of life. These are the sources of renewing the balance and harmony of the world in which we live and of which we are such an inherent part. Moreover, these stories all intend to teach human communities notions of respect for all of the created realm.

In contrast to the Christian story in the Bible, there is no definitive origin story in any Native community. In Hopi traditions, for example, one spirit being (Spider Woman) may make the first human beings and another is called on to give human beings language. While the power of these spirit persons is deeply respected and honored as a manifestation of the Sacred Other, their power is especially appreciated as an ongoing and accessible possibility for us today.[2]

Native traditions generally begin with the existence of a world in some inchoate form, where humans already exist. Thus most Indian storytelling begins with the existence of the world of which we are an integral part. The world in Native traditions begins in the distant past, and Indian intellectual traditions conceive of the world in a constant creative flux that requires our continual participation.

creatio
ex nihilo

Beginnings

several vers.

The beginning of this world and the origins of humanity are the subject of different stories. The people involved in the beginnings of the world are not human persons, even if they seem human enough in the stories that tell of those events. In most traditions, the beginning of the human species comes after the beginning of the earth world.

Typically, each Indian community has a large cycle of stories that are loosely connected and may vary from clan to clan or village to village. Some stories tell of the creation of dry ground in the midst of primordial water. Other stories move on to the creation of day and night or summer and winter. The creation of an island of dirt in the middle of a primordial flood is a story theme that is shared by a great many different tribes from different parts of the continent. These stories are particularly instructive because they assume that there were already

ex nihilo

"people" in the world, before there were human beings. In many of them, this world only emerges after the destruction of an earlier one. In different versions of the story, a variety of these "people"—the otter, the duck, the loon, beaver and turtle, among others—all try to accomplish the impossible, to dive to the bottom of the water and retrieve a little mud for building the first island of land—until the third or fourth attempt is finally successful.

Human Beginnings

There are two general themes in tribal memories in North America about human beginnings: peoples either emerged from below or were crafted from dirt or clay; or they dropped from the sky. The more common theme is that of emergence.

Tohono'oodam tradition remembers that the creator took great pains to make the first two clay figures of humans different from each other, even crafting carefully their genitalia in order that the two might be able to bring pleasure to each other.[3] Hopis, Blackfeet, and others also preserve stories of a human creation from earth, shaped and given life by some creator or spirit person. Pueblos (including Hopis), Choctaws, Lakotas, and others have stories that tell of an emergence of human beings as already whole communities from a world somewhere below the surface of this present world.[4]

Iroquoians and others tell stories of a descent from above.[5] Yet in the Iroquois stories, it is not human beings who make the descent. Rather it is the mother of the "creator" of humans who comes from the sky world. The descent is to a world that is inundated with water from which dry land and a livable world must be created as a first act. The various Iroquois peoples then tell variations of the mud diver story and the formation of this turtle island as a proper home for "Mature Maiden," the pregnant woman who was pushed through the opening of the sky and fell to this world. As the story continues, Mature Maiden gives birth to a daughter who is later impregnated by Wind and gives birth to twins, one good and one evil. It is this good twin who creates human beings out of the clay of the earth.

The Osage stories also tell of a descent from the sky, but the descent is a human one.[6] Sent down to the surface of the earth by Wakonda, the first Osages fell to the earth "like acorns from an acorn tree." Yet these humans were not yet Osages until they met and joined up with a community of humans that were already on the earth and were closely identified with the earth. Those who had descended from the sky formed the basis of the sky division or moiety and were thereafter always referred to as *tzi sho*, or *sky people*. Those with whom they joined formed the basis of the other division of the nation and were thereafter always referred to as *hunka*, or earth people. Because Osage custom required each person to marry someone from the other division, all Osages since this beginning have been both of the earth and of the sky—even though each Osage continues to live as part of one division or the other.[7]

Human Privilege and Communities of Respect

The biblical creation story and the ensuing Christian tradition significantly privilege human beings over the rest of creation. Indeed the relationship stipulated at the beginning of the book of Genesis, as Amer-European readers too commonly interpret it, is one of subjection and domination:

> And God said to them [the humans], "Be fruitful and multiply, and fill the earth and subdue it; and have dominion over the fish of the sea and over the birds of the air and over every living thing that moves upon the earth." (Gen 1:28)

In American Indian cultures human beings are not so privileged in the scheme of things; neither are humans considered external to the rest of the world and its functions. To the contrary, humans are seen as part of the whole, rather than apart from it and free to use it up. Yet there are expectations of human beings. We do have particular responsibilities in the scheme of things, but, then, so do all our other relatives in the created realm: from bears and squirrels to eagles and sparrows, trees, ants, rocks and mountains. In fact, many elders in Indian communities are quick to add that of all the createds, of all our relations, we Two-Leggeds alone seem to be confused as to our responsibility towards the whole.

European Christianity has put humans in opposition to the rest of creation.[8] Kirkpatrick Sale discusses the Medieval European fear of nature and the natural world in his biography of Christopher Columbus. Europeans told fearsome stories about the terrors of the wilderness (nature) and the wild beasts that roamed there. The wilderness was only to be conquered and tamed for cultivation. As Sale suggests, "What it has meant to be 'civilized' since the time of the Myceneans (circa 2000-1100 B.C.E.) has entailed the increasing domination and control of the natural world."[9]

In the course of conquering their fear and taming the wilderness, Europeans deforested much of their landscape from Greco-Roman times onward, using deliberate fires, overgrazing and urban encroachment, a process that continues in many forms today in the United States. This pattern of exploitation begins as early as the time of Aristotle (fourth century B.C.E.), with the birth of so-called objective observation and description, an incipient scientific method. During the European Renaissance, humans became increasingly divorced from the natural world. The Linnean classification system for plants and animals constituted the ultimate sense of domination over the environment—the power to name and categorize all things.

The philosophical and scientific basis for control of nature was initially rooted in the acts of naming. Perhaps the modern Amer-European need for exerting control over the world was most explicitly founded by Descartes in a logical extension of both Aristotle and the Renaissance. Descartes most clearly announced the ultimate knowability of the world and the human responsibility to do the knowing (and hence, exerting control).

This movement towards greater and greater human control over the environment was paralleled by the ever-increasing philosophical and theological importance of the individual in European cultures. The natural world was to be feared as dangerous and unconquered. It was associated with the biblical wilderness, where disorder challenged God's will. The wilderness provided theological reasons for human beings to assert their right and duty to conquer nature and bring it under human control. This privileging of human beings over the rest of creation in Medieval Europe continues to have its affects on Euro-western peoples today.

The philosophical move towards the ascendancy of the individual necessarily included a concomitant displacing of community values. This shift devalued human communities and notions of the common good; but, more important, it displaced spiritual beings as a part of that community. In the Indian intellectual tradition and in cultural practice, human beings are not privileged over the rest of the world, nor are individuals privileged over the good of the whole community.

Balancing the World for Life

Respect for Creation, the whole of the created realm, "all our relations," is vitally important to the well-being of our communities. It is most readily apparent in the general philosophy of balance and harmony, a notion adhered to by all Indian communities in one form or another. Respect for "creation" emerges out of our perceived need for maintaining balance in the world around us. Thus Indian spirituality is characteristically oriented towards balancing of the world and our participation in it both in every-day personal and family actions and the periodic ceremonies of clans, societies, and whole communities. When the balance of existence is disturbed, whole communities pay a price that is measured in some lack of communal well-being.

There are two concepts that we need to understand further

in order to grasp more fully the place of human beings in this on-going process of world balancing and world renewal. The first takes us back to the notion of reciprocity in the opening story of this chapter; the second has to do with spatiality.

Reciprocity: A Foundation for Balance

The American Indian notion of reciprocity is fundamental to all human participation in world-balancing and maintaining harmony. Reciprocity involves first of all an understanding of the cosmos as sacred and alive, and the place of humans in the processes of the cosmic whole. It begins with an understanding that anything and everything that humans do has an effect on the rest of the world around us. Even when we cannot clearly know what that effect is in any particular act, we know that there is an effect. Thus, Indian peoples, in different places and in different cultural configurations, have always struggled to know how to act appropriately in the world. Indeed, this knowledge seems to be the consistent purpose of all Indian creation stories. Knowing that every action has its unique effect has always meant that there had to be some sort of built-in compensation for human actions, some act of reciprocity.

The necessity for reciprocity becomes most apparent where violence is concerned, especially when such violence is an apparent necessity as in hunting or harvesting. Violence cannot be perpetrated, a life taken, in a Native American society, without some spiritual act of reciprocation. I am so much a part of the whole of creation and its balance, anything I do to perpetrate an act of violence, even when it is necessary for the survival of our families and our communities, must be accompanied by an act of spiritual reciprocation intended to restore the balance of existence. It must be remembered that violence as a technical category must extend to all one's "relatives." Thus, a ceremony of reciprocity must accompany the harvesting of vegetable foods such as corn or the harvesting of medicinals such as cedar, even when only part of a plant is taken. The ceremony may be relatively simple, involving a prayer or song and perhaps a reciprocal offering of tobacco.

Many tribes maintained very extensive and complex ceremonies of reciprocation to insure continuing balance and plentiful harvests. Likewise, there is a tradition of mythic stories that accompany such ceremonies and function to provide the theoretical foundation for the ceremonies. Ultimately, all of these stories function further to insure the continuing respect of the communities who tell the stories for all the parts of the created world, all the relatives, upon which the people depend for their own well-being. Even gathering rocks for a purification ceremony (sweat lodge ceremony) calls for care and respect, prayers and reciprocation.

In the same manner, ceremonies involving self-sacrifice (typically called "self-torture" or "self-mutilation" by the missionaries and early ethnographers) also come under this general category of reciprocation. In the Rite of Vigil (vision quest), which is very widespread among Indian peoples of North America, as well as in the Sun Dance, the suffering the supplicant takes upon himself or herself is usually thought of as vicarious and as some sort of reciprocation. Since all of one's so-called possessions are ultimately not possessions but relatives that live with someone, an individual is not giving away a possession when he or she gives a gift to someone else. In actuality the only thing a person really owns and can sacrifice is one's own flesh. Thus these ceremonies of self-sacrifice tend to be the most significant ceremonies of a people.

While missionaries typically thought of these ceremonies as vain human attempts to placate some angry deity, Indian communities know that these ceremonies are much more complex than that. Rather, they are much more often thought of as vicarious sacrifices engaged in for the sake of the whole community's well-being. Moreover, they are thought of as ceremonies that came to the community as a gift from the Sacred Mystery in order to help the community take care of itself and its world. Thus, the Sun Dance is considered a ceremony in which Two-Leggeds participate with the Sacred in order to help maintain life, that is, to maintain the harmony and balance of the whole. All these ceremonies, then, especially those that anthropologists call "world renewal," function as part of the constantly on-going process of creation.

Hunting and war, for example, typically involved a complex ceremonial preparation before a contingent of warriors or hunters left their home. The Osage War Ceremony (nearly identical to the ceremony performed before a buffalo hunt) involved an eleven-day ritual, allowing enough time to affirm the sacredness of life, to consecrate the lives that would be lost in war, and to offer prayers in reciprocation for those potentially lost lives.[10] In the hunt, most Indian nations report specified prayers of reciprocation, involving apologies and words of thanksgiving to the animal itself and the animal's spirit nation. Usually, this ceremonial act is in compliance with the request of the animals themselves as the people remember the primordial negotiations in mythological stories. Thus, formal and informal ceremonies of reciprocation are a day-to-day mythic activity which has its origin in mythological stories in which human beings were given permission by the animal nations to hunt themselves for food. The resulting covenant, however, calls on human beings to assume responsibilities over against the perpetration of violence among Four-Legged relatives. Even after the hunt or battle, those who participated must invariably go through a ceremonial cleansing before re-entering their own village. Not to do this would bring the disruption of the sacred by the perpetration of violence right into the middle of national community life and put all people at risk.[11]

Animals, birds, crops, and medicines are all living relatives and must be treated with respect if they are to be genuinely efficacious for the people. The ideal of harmony and balance requires that all beings respect all other beings, that they respect life and avoid gratuitous or unthinking acts of violence. Maintaining harmony and balance requires that even necessary acts of violence be done "in a sacred way." Thus nothing is taken from the earth without prayer and offering. When the tree is cut down for the Sun Dance, for instance, something must be offered, returned to the spirit world, for the life of that tree. The people not only ceremonially and prayerfully ask its permission but also ask for its cooperation and help during the four days of the dance itself.

American technological and economic development cannot embody the Indian ethic of reciprocity. It is not enough to re-plant a few trees or to add nutrients to the soil. These are superficial acts to treat the negative symptoms of development. The value of reciprocity which is a hallmark of Indian ceremonies goes to the heart of issues of sustainability, which is maintaining a balance and tempering the negative effects of basic human survival techniques. There is no ceremony among any people for clear-cutting an entire forest. → Good thought

Spatiality: Place and Time

Amer-European and American Indian worldviews place quite different values on space and time. Vine Deloria, Jr., the dean of American Indian academics, in his 1972 milestone book: *God Is Red*,[12] and George Tinker[13] argue different cultures orient themselves around either space or time. For Amer-European peoples, time has been the primary category. The ceremonial cycle of Christianity revolves around a seven-day cycle that requires a ceremonial event (mass or liturgies of worship) most typically on the first day of the cycle. The seven-day cycle itself is an arbitrary human convention.

In the Western intellectual tradition, progress, history, development, evolution, and process become key notions in academic discourse. Thus, the Western worldview has an inherent blind spot, which prevents any comprehensive or deep understanding of the scope of ecological devastation which is, in fact, accelerating despite our best efforts at "sustainable development." To do no more than propose "solutions," such as reforestation projects, without acknowledging this blind spot, is only to address the superficial symptoms of mal-development.

In contrast, cultural values, social and political structures in

Indian communities are rooted in a creation worldview shaped by reciprocity and spatiality. Indian ceremonial existence, for instance, is inevitably spatially configured with place taking precedence over the question of when a ceremony will happen. Even in the case of annual or periodic ceremonial cycles, spatial configurations involving spatial relationships between sun or moon and the earth are determinative. Hence the spatial relationship between the community and the sun at solstice or equinox, or the spatial appearance or non-appearance of the moon at full or new moon are more important than calendar dates and Julian months.

This foundational metaphor of spatiality in Indian cultures also begins to clarify the extent to which Indian notions of creation and Indian existence are deeply rooted in our attachment to the land and to specific territories in particular. Each nation has some understanding that they were placed into a relationship with a particular territory by spiritual forces outside of themselves and thus have an enduring responsibility for that territory just as the earth, especially the earth in that particular place, has a filial responsibility toward the people who live there. Likewise, the Two-Legged people in that place also have a spatially related responsibility toward all people who share that place with them, including animals, birds, plants, rocks, rivers, mountains and the like. With knowledge of such extensive kinship ties, including a kinship tie to the land itself, it should be less surprising that Indian peoples have always resisted colonial pressure to relocate them to different territories, to sell their territories to the invaders, or to allow the destruction of their lands for the sake of accessing natural resources. Conquest and removal from our lands, historically, and contemporary ecological destruction of our lands have been and continue to be culturally and genocidally destructive to Indian peoples as peoples.

There is, however, a more subtle level to this sense of spatiality and land-rootedness. It shows up in nearly all aspects of our existence, in our ceremonial structures, our symbols, our architecture, and in the symbolic parameters of a tribe's universe. Hence, the land and spatiality constitute the basic metaphor for existence and determine much of a community's life. In Osage society, for instance, every detail of social structure—even the geographic orientation of the old villages—reflected a reciprocal duality of all that is necessary for sustaining life. Thus the hunka or earth moiety situated to the south of the village and the tzi sho or sky moiety situated to the north represented female and male, matter and spirit, war and peace, but they only functioned fully because they were together and together represented wholeness. Spirit without matter is motion without substance; matter without spirit is motionless and meaningless. Once again we see reciprocity in a symbiotic dualism, this time clearly configured spatially.

We should not think here of the oppositional dualism of good and evil that we have learned to identify as typical Western (i.e., ancient mid-Eastern) dualism. American Indian duality is a necessary reciprocity, not oppositional. They are different manifestations of the same Wakonda, not of two Wakonda even though they carry personality specificity just as traditional Christian trinitarian doctrine would assert. While they are manifestations of the same Wakonda, they are different manifestations, both of which are necessary in order to have some balanced understanding of the Otherness that is the Sacred Mystery. Indeed, Wakonda has manifested itself in a great many other ways, all of which help our people to better understand the Mystery, our world, ourselves and our place in the world. At this point, it may also be clearer why the European word "God" is inadequate to express the full complexity of what we have only begun to explore in the Osage word.

Even the architectural geography of our spirituality functioned politically to give the village group cohesion; it functions at a much more deeply spiritual and social level that still pertains for a great many Indian people today. While an Osage person may be either tzi sho or hunka, she or he is a child of parents who come from each of the divisions. Thus, each individual recognizes herself or himself as a combination of qualities that reflect both sky and earth, spirit and matter, peace and war, male and female, and we struggle individually and communally to hold those qualities in balance with each other. These value structures begin with spatial designs of existence and are rooted in those spatial metaphors as fundamental mores of communal behavior and social organization.

This is not the only spatial symbolic paradigm of existence that determines Native American individuality and community. The fundamental symbol of plains Indian existence is the circle, a polyvalent symbol signifying the family, the clan, the tribe, and eventually all of creation. As a creation symbol, the importance of the circle is its genuine egalitarianness. There is no way to make the circle hierarchical. Because it has no beginning and no end, all in the circle are of equal value. No relative is valued more than any other. A chief is not valued above the people; nor are humans valued above the animal nations, the birds, or even trees and rocks. In its form as a medicine wheel, with two lines forming a cross inscribed vertically and horizontally across its whole, the circle can symbolize the four directions of the earth and, more importantly, the four manifestations of Wakonda that come to us from those directions.

At the same time, for the Osage, the four directions symbolize the four cardinal virtues of the tribe (bravery, generosity, humility, and honesty), the sacred powers of four animal nations, and the four racial nations that walk the earth (Black, Red, White, and Yellow). In the Osage conception of the universe, all human beings walk ideally in egalitarian balance. Other tribes express egalitarian ideals in similar spatial symbolism.

At one level of meaning, the four directions hold together in the same egalitarian balance the four nations of Two-Leggeds, Four-Leggeds, Wingeds, and Living-Moving Things. In this model of the universe, human beings lose their status of primacy and "dominion." Implicitly and explicitly, American Indians are driven by their culture and spirituality to recognize the personhood of all things in creation.

Western concepts of temporality and historicity lend themselves implicitly to hierarchy of knowledge because someone with a greater investment of time may know more of the body of temporally codified knowledge. Knowledge of terrain and space is part of general human experience.

[handwritten: open sentence]

The Circle and Mitakuye Oyasin

American Indians and other indigenous peoples have a long-standing confidence that they have much to teach Europeans and North Americans about the world and human relationships in the world. They are confident in the spiritual foundations of their insights, confident that those foundations can become a source of healing and reconciliation for all Creation.

Our Indian ancestors had a relationship with God as Creator that was healthy and responsible long before they knew of or confessed the Gospel of Jesus Christ. They had a relationship with Creator that was solidified in the stories they told around the camp fires in each of our tribes, in their prayers, and especially in their ceremonies. This relationship began with the recognition of the Other as Creator, the creative force behind all things that exist, and long predated the coming of the missionaries. In that relationship, the people saw themselves as participants within Creation as a whole, as a part of Creation, and they celebrated the balance and harmony of the whole of the universe in all that they did together.

In all that they did our Indian ancestors acknowledged the goodness of the Creator and of all Creation including themselves. That was the point of the stories, the focus of their prayers, and the purpose of the ceremonies. They recognized the balance and harmony that characterized all of the created universe: winter and summer were held in balance with one another. So also were hunting and planting, sky and earth, hot and cold, sun and moon, female and male, women and men. Our ancestors recognized all this as good, just as does the voice of God at the end of the sixth day in Genesis 1:31.

We have already suggested that each Indian national com-

[handwritten left margin: Always had "god" relationship]

munity tells a variety of creation stories. Once while visiting a reservation community, one of the authors asked one of the local storytellers if he would tell their creation story. His first response was to decline because, as he put it, there was not enough time to tell the story. It usually takes four days he said, just to tell one story. Finally, convinced that an abbreviated version might work for this non-member of the community, he thought for a moment and said, "I will summarize for you the version that my aunt taught me." When asked exactly how many versions of the creation story there were, he responded that he personally had been given four different versions which he was authorized to tell. At least this Indian visitor did not try to ask, "Which one is the true version." As most Indians already know, the answer is that all of them are true—in different ways and for different occasions.

The Bible is really no different than this story suggests about American Indian oral traditions. Some years ago, a Bible teacher from one of the mainline seminaries was subpoenaed to testify in a court case brought by fundamentalist Christians who wanted "creationism" taught in public schools. When he was asked how many different creation stories there were in the Old Testament, this scholar answered, "Five." Five different creation stories in the Bible?! Yet it can be demonstrated, for instance, that Genesis 1 and Genesis 2 are really very different stories dating back to the time before they were written down, when they were a part of the Israelite oral tradition.[14] The different order in which creation occurs in these two chapters is enough to convince most objective readers that the two are different and must be understood quite apart from each other rather than harmonized into some unified story just in order to preserve some doctrinal "integrity" of Scripture. Genesis 1 lists the order of creation day-by-day with animals and human beings both being created on the last day. Yet it is important for Genesis 1 that animals are created first, leaving human beings to be created as the very last of God's creative acts, the jewel of creation, created in the image of God. Human beings are also important in Genesis 2, but the order of creation is decidedly different, since human beings are created before the animals, and the animals are created in order to find an appropriate partner for the human being.

If all American Indian spiritual insights and hence Indian theology must begin with Creation, these stories already exist in the basic liturgical posture of Indians in many North American tribes. Except where our communities have been thoroughly evangelized by European culture, our prayers are most often said with the community assembled into some form of circle.

In fact, the circle is a key symbol for self-understanding in these tribes, representing the whole of the universe and our part in it. We see ourselves as co-equal participants in the circle standing neither above nor below anything else in God's Creation. There is no hierarchy in our cultural context, even of species, because the circle has no beginning nor ending. Hence all the createds participate together, each in their own way, to preserve the wholeness of the circle.

When a group of Indians forms a circle to pray, all know that the prayers have already begun with the representation of a circle. No words have yet been spoken and in some ceremonies no words need be spoken, but the intentional physicality of our formation has already expressed our prayer and deep concern for the wholeness of all of God's Creation. There is no need to hold hands because we know it is enough to stand in the circle already joined together, inextricably bound, through the earth which lies firm beneath our feet, the earth who is, after all, the true mother of each of us and of all Creation.

The Lakota and Dakota peoples have a phrase used in all their prayers that aptly illustrates the Native American sense of the centrality of creation. The phrase, *mitakuye oyasin*, functions somewhat like the word "amen" in European and American Christianity. As such, it is used to end every prayer, and often it is in itself a whole prayer, being the only phrase spoken. The usual translation offered is: "For all my relations." Yet like most Native symbols, *mitakuye oyasin* is polyvalent in its meaning. Certainly, one is praying for one's immediate family:

aunts, cousins, children, grandparents, etc. "Relations" must also be understood as fellow tribal members or even all Indian people. At the same time, the phrase includes all the nations of Two-Leggeds in the world and, in the ever-expanding circle, all the nations other than Two-Leggeds—the Four-Leggeds, the Wingeds and all the Living-Moving Things of the Earth.

A translation of *mitakuye oyasin* would better read: "For all the above me and below me and around me things." That is, for all my relations. It is this inter-relatedness that best captures what might symbolize for Indian peoples what Amer-Europeans would call creation. More to the point, it is this understanding of inter-relatedness, of balance and mutual respect of the different species in the world, that characterizes what we might call Indian peoples' greatest gift to Amer-Europeans and to the Amer-European understanding of creation at this time of world ecological crisis.

Perhaps one can begin to understand the extensive image of inter-relatedness and interdependence symbolized by the circle and the importance of reciprocity and respect for one another for maintaining the wholeness of the circle. The American Indian concern for starting theology with Creation is a need to acknowledge the goodness and inherent worth of all of God's creatures.

Chapter 3

DEITY

The Creative Power in the World

Your missionary ancestors told Indian people that they were worshipping a false god when we pray to the sun. The sun is the most powerful physical presence in our lives. Without it we could not live and our world would perish. Yet our reverence for it, our awe, was considered idolatry.

But your missionary ancestors misunderstood even that much, because we never worshipped the sun. We merely saw in it the reflection of the sacred, the creator, and used its image to focus our prayers of thanksgiving for Creator's life-giving power. It is, for us, a constant reminder of the creative power of God, as we greet the sun in the morning when we first arise and again in the evening. In between, as we go about our day, we constantly will see our shadow on the ground and will be reminded again of God's creative goodness. We can stop, look up, and say a short prayer whenever this happens.

Phillip Deere, 1984

Native traditions that survive in modern practice and under-standing can inform our understanding and interpretation of the earlier evidence collected by ethnographers. Indian practice has certainly changed over the centuries since European contact. Any two cultures which live side by side will develop some intimacy that results in borrowing of traditions and parts of traditions from each other. This is bound to be the case especially where one culture is dominated economically and militarily by the other. The continuity of practice is, however, greater than has generally been conceded by scholars.

The nature of deity among Native people in North America has been the subject of scholarly discussion.[1] Issues include the applicability or inapplicability of categories such as polytheism or monotheism;[2] questions of animism or animatism;[3] the presumed lack of systematic specificity about these beliefs;[4] and the very applicability of categories such as "god" or "supernatural."[5]

Diverse Cultural Views of God and Gods

To begin to understand notions of deity in Indian cultures requires the fundamental recognition of the importance of metaphoric language in these tribes. God appears in many forms apparent in the environment. Descriptions of nature embed an understanding of spiritual power in descriptions of natural events. This fact can somewhat account for Åke Hultkranz's perception of concepts only "vaguely delimited," as well as for James Walker's continuing confusion after nearly two decades of dedicated effort on the Pine Ridge reservation.[6]

A common conception is that Indians worshipped the earth as a goddess. Although documentary evidence does not support such a belief among Indian tribes at the time of European contact (where written records originated), it appeared in romanticized notions of Indian cultures in the early nineteenth century. The Shawnee leader Tecumseh, in his attempt to promote a pan-Indian alliance to drive whites from Indian lands, adopted the terminology of earth as mother and spread it among tribes that he visited.[7] American Indian peoples did not originally worship the Earth as a goddess. But just as assuredly, they always have and still do recognize the earth as a living be-ing, as a relative, as generative of life, as sacred, and often as mother or grandmother.[8]

The academic study of deity raises methodological issues. The first is the general trustworthiness of early documentary evidence. The second is the practice of ethnographers to create categories of human experience and understanding that become standards for subsequent scholarship. The third is the problem of language and translation.

For the most part up to the present Indian peoples have lacked the linguistic tools in English to explain the great complexity of their tribal beliefs and ways. In many cases Indian spokespeople failed to understand what it was that their new Anglo neighbors didn't understand, or were not, themselves, prepared to understand, more or less the same error Amer-Europeans have consistently made in their attempts to acculturate (civilize) and proselytize Native Americans.

Some categories of knowledge are so basic that they are simply assumed, most often unconsciously, in explaining other categories of existence that may be more consciously disparate. It is likely that pervasive Indian categories of existence were not explicitly stated in statements about basic beliefs. For example, James Dorsey was a gifted linguist, and his manners ingratiated him to Indian people; Dorsey nevertheless fails to note the directional orientation of Osage, Lakota, and other Siouan camps. Preferring to speak of the left and right side where moiety division of a village or camp occurs, he invariably draws each camp circle as if the dividing line ran from south to north with the opening to the north. Today it is well known that Lakota and Osage camps opened to the east and that in the case of the Osages the line dividing the moieties followed the path of the sun from east to west.[9] Why this fact went unnoticed by Dorsey, why he evidently did not ask about directional orientation, or why his informants for whom the issue was demonstrably important withheld this vital information must remain something of a mystery. What we can, with hind sight, say is that Dorsey's work was remarkable as far as it went but was severely limited, this in spite of Dorsey's abilities to break down much of the protective reticence to reveal sacred information.

Dorsey includes a revealing paragraph apropos this latter concern.[10] With respect to the difficulty in learning the names of the different clans in a tribe, because of the sacredness of those names, Dorsey says:

> Such names are never used in ordinary conversation. This is especially the case in tribes where the secret society continues in all its power, as among the Osage, the Ponka, and the Kansa. When the author was questioning these Indians he was obliged to proceed very cautiously in order to obtain information of this character, which was not communicated till they learned about his acquaintance with some of the myths. When several Dakota delegations visited Washington he called on them and had little trouble in learning the names of their gentes, their order in the camping circle, etc., provided the interpreters were absent. During his visit to the Omaha, from 1878 to 1880, he did not find them very reticent in furnishing him with such information, though he was generally referred to the principal chief of each gens as the best authority for the names in his own division. But he found it very difficult to induce any of them to admit that the gentes had subdivisions, which were probably the original gentes. It was not till 1880, and after questioning many that by the merest accident he obtained the clew from the keeper of a sacred pipe.[11]

Were Indian tribes originally polytheistic or monotheistic, or put another way, did Indian tribes have a notion of a "high God"? Paul Radin's studies indicate the complexity of the debate and Radin's own vacillation on the question.[12] Initially he proposed that the Pawnee provided "an example of primitive monotheism," a view that he later repudiated.[13]

The translation of the term "god" in native languages is problematic. The only word listed in the Osage dictionary un-

worship = ceremony

der "God" (there is no entry for "god") is Wako^{n}da.[14] Likewise in Buechel's Lakota dictionary the translation offered for "wakantanka" is "God, the Supreme Being."[15] Obviously both translations are glossic presumptions and categoric impositions. To carry the critique a step further, Indian ceremonial life is rarely characterized as "worship" by Indian people. Usually contemporary Indian people refer to their community rituals (clan, tribe, district, region, etc.) simply as "ceremonies." Some ceremonies are "dances" as in the Sun Dance. Many Navajo ceremonies are "sings." Pueblos call some of their ceremonies "feast days"; Native American Church calls its ceremonies "meetings." Yet in each case "ceremony" is an acceptable English signification. Worship would in each case be awkward, only occasionally adopted by Indian speakers as a gloss carried over from the missionary experience. And, indeed, what happens in these ceremonies, as diverse as they are from each other, is perceived by contemporary Indians as categorically different from the complex connoted by the word worship.

The key ingredient in worship missing in Indian ceremonies is any element of praise. While thankfulness is crucial,[16] along with commitment and prayer, praise for the Mysterious Other, the spirit world, Creator, or whatever seems wholly unnecessary in the Indian context. Because Indian people in their traditional beliefs see themselves as participating in an ongoing relationship with the spirits, praise is inappropriate because it implies a sense of individual ego that does not exist in Native beliefs.

Wako^{n}da: An Indian Deity

Wako^{n}da is the expression of deity for the Osage people in Oklahoma. Wako^{n}da informs the contemporary practice of the Ilonshka dances that are held in the communities of Grey Horse and Pawhuska in northeast Oklahoma. Earlier versions of the Ilonshka are drawn from texts recorded and translated by Francis LaFlesche, a member of the Omaha tribe, a tribe closely related to the Osages. LaFlesche's texts as written documents explain Osage cosmology and its working out in village and tribal structure. Wakoⁿda is the word used by the early missionaries to express the Christian concept of God, and, indeed, LaFlesche offers God as one English translation. Treated thus, however, both words are simply used as popular glosses.

LaFlesche's second entry begins to get at the real heart of the matter: Wakoⁿda, is the name applied by the Osage to the mysterious, invisible, creative power which brings into existence all living things of whatever kind. They believe that this great power resides in the air, the blue sky, the clouds, the stars, the sun, the moon, and the earth, and keeps them in motion.[17]

The Osage world was (is) one of thorough-going dualism. The diametric dualism is still readily apparent in multiple and polyvalent ways. Indian cultures almost universally depend upon divisions within their communities to structure social relationships. Like the Omahas, Poncas, Quapaws, and others, the Osage tribe and its encampment was divided into two parts:[18] the Tsi Zhu, or Sky People division, and the Hoⁿ'ga or Earth People division, with mandated cross-divisional marriage. The encampment (both permanent towns and hunting camps) was divided by an east-west roadway, the Tsi Zhu constructing their lodges to the north and the Hoⁿ'ga to the south. This spatial arrangement is repeated in the seating of the Noⁿhoⁿzhiⁿga, the council of elders, inside a lodge prepared for ceremonial observance.

Much of the cosmological mythology of the tribe consists of accounts of the different origin of the two divisions and how they came to be together. Indeed, the Tsi Zhu division has its origins in the sky itself where they were created as incorporeal entities who then needed to attain corporeality. In this process they are eventually sent down to earth by Wakoⁿda, dropping like acorns from an oak tree. In their wanderings on the earth they soon discover the Hoⁿ'ga, the isolated earth people. After some negotiation these two decide to live together as one, bringing together the distinct qualities of each, both symbolically and functionally representing the whole of the Osage cosmology. Mandated intermarriage functions to hold the two divisions together. It also holds together the universe in microcosm and brings the opposites together both in the whole and in each individual.

In the Ton-won-a-don-be wi-gi-e, a Nonhonzhinga (council of elders) ceremony that marks the beginning of a new year and was observed around the spring equinox, appeal was made to the four winds and to what LaFlesche translates "the four great gods" of the Osage, two pairs each in reciprocal relationship to the other.[19] In this case, Wa'-kon-da gthon-the do-ba' (lines 7 and again line 8) can be more neutrally translated:

There are four great Wa'konda:
>   Hon'-ba Wa-çu. . . Wi-tsi-go e' . . .   (lines 11f)
>   The god of the cloudless days . . . Grandfather . . .
>   Wa'-kon-da Hon-non-pa- çe. . . I-ko e' . . .   (lines 30f)
>   The goddess of darkness . . . Grandmother . . .
>   Wa'-kon-da Mon-shi-ta . . . Wi-tsi-go e' . . . (lines 50f)
>   The god of the upper region (sky) . . . Grandfather . . .
>   Wa-kon-da hui-dse-ta . . . I-ko e' . . .   (lines 64f)
>   The goddess of the lower region (earth) . . .
>   Grandmother . . .

The second pair is particularly important—Wa'-kon-da Mon-shi-ta and Wa'-kon-da hui-dse-ta, Wakonda above and Wakonda below, that is sky and earth. What LaFlesche already knew, apparent from comments in other contexts, is that these four are certainly not gods, even though his translation clearly says exactly that: An earth goddess called grandmother and a sky god called grandfather. Here we see reflected in Wakonda the same cosmological structure that was patterned in the tribe's mythology and in the architecture of the encampment.

Osage testimony—both ancient and contemporary—recognizes that Wakonda is one. To quote again from LaFlesche's Osage dictionary: "Sometimes the Osage speak of a tree, a rock, or a prominent hill as Wakonda, but when asked if his people had great numbers of Wakondas he would reply, 'Not so; there is but

No praise

metaphors

one God and His presence is in all things and everywhere. We say a tree is Wakoⁿda because in it also Wakoⁿda resides."[20] Yet the unity of Wakoⁿda must here be held in tension with fourness and the clear ritual proclamation that there are four Wakoⁿda. Fourness and unity are not necessarily at odds. One becomes four as Osage people perceive Wakoⁿda as manifesting itself in various ways. In this case the manifestations of Wakoⁿda are metaphorically represented as light and dark, sky and earth, two pairs manifest as male/female reciprocity. At the same time LaFlesche attests to Wakoⁿda as unitary and invisible, continuing his dictionary entry with a lengthy story retold from the oral tradition of the tribe. Wakoⁿda is manifest in sky and earth and yet is patently unmanifest.[21]

The Lakota likewise see Wakan Tanka manifest in a variety of ways in the world. Each of these very different manifestations can actually be referred to as Wakan Tanka, and yet Wakan Tanka is, in another sense, all of them. This is apparent in the material collected by J. R. Walker during his eighteen years as staff physician on the Pine Ridge Reservation from 1896 to 1914.[22] Walker diagrams the basic structure of Wakan Tanka in a way that reflects what is still taught among Lakota people today.

Yet it needs to be said that it is never actually taught in the systematic way that Walker relates. Walker speaks of four ranks of form (Tob Tob Kin) each of which is Wakan Tanka and all of which is Wakan Tanka. The first rank includes the four key figures in the Lakota creation myth: Wi (sun), Skan (sky), Maka (earth), and Inyan (rock). While Sun is paired reciprocally with Moon (Hanwi, in the second rank), it becomes clear in many contexts that sky and earth are also paired.

An example of this occurs in the Four Directions Song, a ceremonial song still used in a variety of ceremonial contexts (sweat lodge, pipe ceremony, Yuwipi, etc.). The first four verses are sung to invoke the grandfathers (Tunkasila) of the four directions. The final two verses are sung respectively to the above and the Earth (Maka), grandmother.

Walker, of course, calls each manifestation of Wakan Tanka

"god." But that translation clouds over even the complexity that Walker himself had come to understand and implicitly reduces Lakota thought to some sort of polytheism. The real complexity of Lakota thought might be hinted at as unity expressed in diversity. To Lakota Peoples each manifestation is Wakan Tanka, yet does not exhaust Wakan Tanka. As Little Wound reported to Walker, "Wakan Tanka are many. But they are all the same as one. . . . The Sun is Wakan Tanka, and the Sky and the Earth and the Rock. They are Wakan Tanka."[23] Or again, from a conversation in 1905 with George Sword, Bad Wound, No Flesh and Thomas Tyon (serving as interpreter), Walker's notes record: "Wakan Tanka is like sixteen different persons. But each person is kan. Therefore they are all only the same as one."[24]

Throughout the evidence reported by Walker, Maka is consistently identified as Wakan Tanka and as Grandmother. There are occasions when offerings are made especially to Maka[25] and occasions when particular appeal is made to her for help.[26] Maka is the first of all creation, emanating from pre-existent Inyan (Rock), and as such Maka is ancestor, generative source, or, as Walker reports, "grandmother of all things."[27] This could easily lead any English speaker to identify Maka as goddess, or Wi (Sun) or Skan (sky) as gods. Indeed, each is Wakan Tanka, but Wakan Tanka is only one.

Åke Hultkranz, like Paul Radin, underwent a shift in his thinking about plains Indians theistic notions. In a late essay on Shoshone and Lakota (he calls them Dakota) notions, he argues for what he calls "unqualified theism," in which "different vaguely delimited concepts exist side by side."[28] He poses three possible forms in which unqualified theism might occur—namely, a vertical structure in which a high god presides over the lesser gods; a horizontal structure in which the various gods or spirits participate equally even if a high god is identified; and a more amorphous structure where the varieties of gods together constitute the essence of a high god. Hultkranz dismisses this third option out of hand and identifies an alternation between the other two for both Shoshone and Lakota depending on circumstances. Yet in my understanding the dismissed option may come closer to describing the experience of both Osage and Lakota peoples—then and now.

If the unity in diversity of sixteen Wakan Tanka seems overwhelming, it can be demonstrated that even this does not exhaust Wakan Tanka, but Wakan Tanka like Wakoⁿda is to be found everywhere and in all things. While the material world is not to be confused with Wakan Tanka or Wakoⁿda, they are infused in all things, even if only manifest or recognized in some. Most commonly today in Lakota belief, Wakan Tanka's power is most often immediately experienced in the presence of "spirits." In contemporary Lakota prayers petitions are repeatedly addressed to Tunkasila (Grandfather). Lakota, like Osage, has no general plural form.[29] Typically a medicine man (wicasa wakan) will function as interpreter for up to several hundred different spirits, which may include one or more of the sixteen Tob Tob Kin.[30]

Like the Christian mystery of the holy trinity, the Lakota mystery of Wakan is complex. The manifestations of the Christian God in the Father, Son, and Holy Ghost can be stated as emotional and intellectual states—creative, giving, and communicative. The manifestations of Wakan are the physical forces in the environment—the sun and moon, the blue of the sky, things that move, like wind, and things that endure, like rock. These are forces that are readily discernible and accessible to Indian people. For Indian Christians, they reside beside the more intangible elements of Christian belief.

CHAPTER 4

CHRISTOLOGY[1]

Who Do You Say That I Am?

"What can the death of a man 2000 years ago possibly have to do with people who live today?" This serious theological question was posed by a man who had been raised a Christian Indian, but had begun incorporating traditional spiritual practices, including the Sun Dance, back into his life for several years. For the moment, however, there was an answer for him that slowed him down even if only temporarily. "Why do you dance?" was the question asked in return. Sometimes the deepest theological discussions are very short and to the point. His only reply was, "Oh!... Yeah." No more words were needed, since both Indians knew full well the vicarious suffering aspect of Indian spiritual commitments at Sun Dance, the Rite of Vigil, and the Purification Ceremony (called sweat lodge in English, by some).

told by George "Tink" Tinker

"Who do you say that I am?" The question Jesus asks of his disciples in the Synoptic Gospels has become the most enduring question of Christian life, in terms of the faith of individuals, of the character of denominations, and of Christian intellectual discourse. An American Indian theology must also make some attempt to address the question, and we do here in two different ways. First we will discuss how some customary Euro-Christian language is inappropriate for American Indian communities and suggest that there might be more appropriate metaphors, both scriptural and indigenous, for referencing Jesus and the Christ in a Christian Indian context. Secondly, however, we will move to re-evaluate the suitability or appropriateness of even this project in the healing process of a colonized community damaged socially, emotionally and spiritually by the past five hundred years of conquest and destruction. Many Indian people have been missionized and continue to find personal solace in their connection with the church, and the first part of this chapter may help them to rediscover a more culturally appropriate christology for an Indian church. A great many others, however, have found any affirmation of the Christ of Christianity to be merely another imposition of colonial control. This essay is a small exercise in neo-colonial resistance in search of genuine American Indian liberation, part of a much broader quest engaging Indian peoples today. This chapter intends to speak somehow to both colonizer and colonized about the nature of christology.

The Gift of Vicarious Suffering

Virtually every tribal nation in North America has had a variety of ceremonies whereby the individual might take on a discipline of vicarious suffering for the sake of the people as a whole. In every case, the first European and Amer-European invaders of indigenous lands, including especially the missionaries, mistook the intentions of these ceremonies. Predicated on misunderstanding, sometimes very intentionally, the missionaries and the Amer-European government proceeded to condemn ancient Native rites as devil worship or idolatry. Yet, these ceremonies have much in common with the suffering of

Jesus in the Christian gospels, because the individual undertaking the ceremony willingly undergoes a discipline of suffering on behalf of the people. This is even true in the case of the Rite of Vigil, often called the "vision quest" in the literature. While there are particularly individual benefits that can accrue from engaging in this ceremony of fasting and prayer, even the eventual benefits are enjoyed by the individual for the sake of the community as a whole.[2]

Because of their understanding of vicarious suffering in such ceremonial contexts, Indian people have an inherent insight into the Christian concept of grace that precedes the arrival of the missionaries. We could even go so far as to insist that we already knew the gospel! However, the missionaries had a vested interest in separating Indian people from their ancient ceremonial structures and consistently taught that these ceremonies fell far short of the Christian ideal. Such practices were, the missionaries insisted, merely vain human attempts to placate an angry god—an impossibility in the first place, went the message, and unnecessary in the light of God's grace revealed in the gospel of Jesus Christ. Contemporary Indians are today realizing that the missionary interpretation was a self-serving lie, a colonial act of domination.

There is no sense in any Native traditions that reflect any attempt to make God, a god or the spirits happy with us or to placate the judgment of God over against a sinful humanity. There is no sense of God's anger. In fact, the notion of Wakonda cannot conceive of ascribing human emotions to Wakonda. Yet, we do conceive of Wakonda as functioning in the best interests of the created world. We know Wakonda, however, much more as a sacred but impersonal force that only becomes personified in order to facilitate human understanding. Ceremonies were given in order that humans might do their share as Two-Leggeds in maintaining the world, just as all other species contribute their part. Thus Native communities participate with Wakonda, the Sacred Energy or Mystery or Power. Likewise we participate with the more personified spirits that are part of Wakonda's self-manifestation.

There were and are ceremonies to make right an imbalance that we ourselves as pitiful two-leggeds may have instigated—through our laziness, inattention, oversight, anger, or some unknown mistake. But even in such cases, the anger of the spirits is never at stake in most Native traditions when those traditions are understood at their most complex level. The spirits are, rather, neutral and follow a natural, pre-determinable course. We are mere players in this drama and have been given ceremonies and ways of being that can help to determine the outcome. Thus, Native ceremonies are gifts to Indian communities, signs of what Euro-Christian theology would call God's grace, or the intrinsic goodness of Wakonda and all of its various manifestations and personifications as Grandmothers and Grandfathers.

If our native ways already had some notion of God's Good News, then it becomes important for us to preserve this original wisdom rather than blindly consume alien notions of the "Good News" imposed by the missionaries. Otherwise, the cost to Native peoples is the loss of cultural values which sustained an inculturated sense of community and personal self-esteem.

American Indians and Jesus

Given the implicit and explicit participation of the churches' missionaries in the oppression and cultural genocide of American Indians, what relevance can Jesus have for Indian peoples? How can Native preachers proclaim Jesus to a community that has been constantly hurt by the proclamation of the gospel and those who have proclaimed it? The initial problem is not with Jesus but with Christianity and the church. Secondly, if Jesus is not necessarily a problem, language about Jesus can be quite problematic. The churches might reasonably make a linguistic/theological shift that would be more inclusive of Indian peoples and their cultures and values. In the final analysis, however, the historical experience of colonization and conquest may continue to make any use of Jesus problematic for American Indian peoples. It is difficult for many Indians to concede efficacy to a system of religious belief which has consistently, over several generations, proven to be an intimate and symbiotic part of the conquest and the ongoing colonial presence.

Traditional spiritual elders, medicine women and men, rather consistently expressed their respect for Jesus as a spiritual person and even as a manifestation of the Creator (namely, God, or something like what Amer-Europeans mean by God). While these spiritual elders and medicine people may have significant resistance to Church and to Christianity, they can respect Jesus as having been a spiritual presence and even as a continuing spiritual presence in the world. As these elders have expressed themselves, Jesus is much more acceptable than the Church.

Some find it curious that when traditional people, including medicine people, come to Indian churches, they find it relatively easy to participate in those ceremonial "services of worship." There are several reasons why this happens relatively easily. 1) Traditional values often dictate that spiritual respect for another's ceremony supersedes one's political conviction. 2) For many there is a recognition of spiritual power in Jesus that goes beyond ethnicity or culture and is similar to the spiritual power already experienced in traditional Indian ceremonial life. 3) There is a traditional valuing of shared hospitality: when in someone else's camp, one does what they do. 4) Most importantly, many were simply expressing a sense of solidarity with those Indian people who have been converted to Christianity by participating occasionally with them. Among these elders there is a sense that those who have remained with the traditional ways or returned to them cannot abandon converted Indians as if they no longer belong to the community. The Indian concern for community will not permit the individual to exclude others from the group.

In any case, the distinction between these traditional people's response to Jesus and the Church or Christianity as an institution is critical. They have largely screened out Christian language about Jesus and focused only on the mythic person. This is important because so many Indian people have been missionized and continue as members of main-line denominations. One response to the problem of language, then, is to search for more culturally appropriate translations of metaphors. We propose here a project of contextualizing and inculturating theology. In the interests of American Indian Christians, one might propose the development of an American Indian christology which would make Jesus more authentically accessible to Indian people. This process might begin by identifying existing Euro-Christian language that is unhelpful or even destructive. One example of this latter is the common Christian reference to Jesus as Lord.

Language and Lordship: Jesus as Conqueror

For the World Council of Churches, the proclamation that "Jesus is Lord" is the doctrinal glue, the bare bones common confession, that holds all the churches together. It is standard Euro-Christian christological language. Yet the colonial oppressiveness of the proclamation is little noted, even by Indian peoples. The cultural otherness of the language used in this common confession once again means that American Indian peoples are being co-opted into a cultural frame of reference that necessitates self-denial and assimilation to the language and social structures of the conqueror.

As foundational as this confession is for many Euro-Christians, it is the one scriptural metaphor used for the Christ event that is ultimately unacceptable and even hurtful to American Indian peoples. There was no analogue in North American indigenous societies for the relationship of power and disparity which is usually signified by the word "lord." To the contrary, North American cultures and social structures were fundamentally marked by their egalitarian nature. Even a so-called "chief" had typically very limited authority which even then depended much on the person's charismatic stature within the community and skill at achieving consensus. The American Indian experiential knowledge of lordship only begins with the conquest and colonization of our nations at the onslaught of the European invasion. What Indians know about lords and lordship, even today, has more to do with the hierarchies of power resulting from colonization. Unfortunately, by extension, even the church becomes a part of these new colonial relationships, with lords in the form of bishops and missionaries (both male and female) to whom Indians have learned as conquered peoples to pay lordly deference.

To call upon Jesus as Lord within this context is a classic example of the colonized participating in our own oppression. To call upon Jesus as Lord is to concede the colonial reality of new hierarchical social structures; it is to concede the conquest as final and become complicit in the ongoing genocidal death of our peoples.[3] It is an act of the colonized mind blindly reciting words that the colonizer has taught—which violate our own cultures but bring great comfort to the lordly colonizer and his missionaries.

Lordship and the Shaping of the Amer-European Experience

Some will object that the lordship metaphor for Christ is actually helpful for White, Amer-European Christians, because it puts many into a posture of humble surrender to another, a posture to which most are quite unaccustomed. Yet, the metaphor does exactly the opposite. It is ultimately not helpful for Amer-European Christians any more than it is for American Indians. Rather, the metaphor seems to excuse White Amer-Europeans from any earthly humility or surrender, and to facilitate often a lack of consciousness with regard to the impropriety of relationships of exploitation. Since one has surrendered as an individual to an overwhelmingly powerful numinous Other, no other surrender or act of humility is called for within the human community. Indeed, many Amer-European

Christians seem to feed on a hierarchical view of the world which has historically privileged and continues to privilege White people on this continent and in other Third World colonial contexts. Thus, rather than being humbled in submission, they are empowered and emboldened—sometimes even explicitly empowered for imposing their own brand of submission on others. Having submitted to the lordship of Jesus, there is no longer any earthly authority to which one must submit or pay homage. Indeed, humbled as a vassal before Jesus, one becomes empowered as Jesus' champion in the world, a soldier for Christ. Unfortunately, the correlation of this notion with White superiority and White privilege regularly serves White political and economic interests as well, defining those interests as somehow naturally concurrent with the interests of God.

Moreover, "Lord" is one of those biblical metaphors that seems to have lost all symbolic cognitive moorings in modern American society. The problem is that there are no "lords" in our society and no use of "lord" as a form of address that might conceivably give the metaphor content. Indeed, any use of the word in the United States today is an anachronistic metaphor requiring the hearer to summon up memories of historical uses of the word in English history and literature that predates the American Revolution, or it requires a cross-cultural understanding of the living anachronism in contemporary English society. Like the language of the "kingdom of God," these persistent metaphors from the first-century Mediterranean world require that modern North Americans must engage in enough of a linguistic-cultural history lesson to have some idea what the word might have meant in the past before they can appropriate any spiritual content from the proclamation of Jesus as Lord for the present.

Modern biblical exegesis is an on-going attempt to recover meanings in the biblical texts from research in ancient biblical societies and languages. Thus exegesis would attempt to explicate the lordship metaphor in terms of the social and political arrangements that dictated the use of language in Palestine and

[handwritten margin note: No lords in AZ society]

the Greco-Roman world of the Christian gospels. This, however, does not solve the problem that the most accessible use of the word for Amer-Europeans (and undoubtedly for many of the rest of us because of our experience of colonialism in America) is not its use in the eastern Mediterranean world of Jesus' day, but rather its use in European cultures which continues to some extent even today—in places like England, for instance, which still maintains in Parliament a House of Lords. Yet the European use of the word, rooted as it is in the social structures of medieval feudalism, is in actuality a far cry from the Palestinian (Aramaic) use that would have been familiar to Mark or even the Hellenistic (Greco-Roman) use that would have been the experience of Luke.

What we are experiencing is a shift away from the useful, meaningful, experiential use of language, to what can only be categorized as "religious language." And it can be further argued that religious language is, by definition and de facto, language that has lost its meaning; that is, religious language has no currency of meaning in the day-to-day, real world use of language. Religious language is made up of old language usages that now continue to have meanings only in so far as they continue to function in that small slice of modern life reserved for religion.

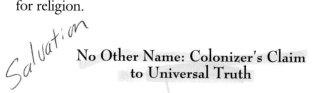

No Other Name: Colonizer's Claim to Universal Truth

Many would insist that the American Indian case for spiritual self-determination can and must be made on its own merits without recourse to Amer-European concepts. While Indian peoples have a spiritual understanding of the world which is inherently amenable to some central Christian concepts, such as grace, we must understand Indian spiritual traditions in their own right and in their own uniqueness. They are not spiritual "puzzle pieces" which can be locked into a universal Christian truth, but have their own meaning and vibrancy within each discrete Indian culture. On the other hand, for the sake of those Indian people who have made a lasting commitment to the colonizer's religious traditions and have converted to Christianity, it can be important to demonstrate the plausibility of Indian religious traditions on the basis of an indigenous interpretation of the colonizer's own texts. Two of those texts take on an enriched meaning when interpreted with a different eye than most Amer-European or European biblical scholars would bring to the task. The first text is from the Acts of the Apostles (4:10, 12), where Peter is responding to the questioning of the court:

Salvation

> Be it known to you all, and to all the people of Israel, that by the name of Jesus Christ of Nazareth, whom you crucified, whom God raised from the dead, by him this man is standing before you well.... And there is salvation in no one else, for there is no other name under heaven given among human beings by which we must be saved.

Salvation for ancestors

Based upon this text, several theological and socio-political problems become immediately apparent for Indian peoples. First, an Indian Christian can be saved today because God sent White people to bring the gospel, but what about that person's ancestors—if salvation is only by the name of Jesus or, in the Catholic version, only in the church? All our Indian ancestors were directly accused of engaging in Devil worship by the earliest European invaders of Indian lands, and, unfortunately, classical Christian doctrine holds out little hope for their joining any converted Christian Indian in the afterlife (in heaven). According to the gospel taught by the missionaries, in heaven Christian Indians will be separated from our pagan ancestors and will live for eternity in a world ("new heaven and new earth") populated primarily by our conquerors and colonizers. *Sad!*
Secondly, and more immediately pressing, Christian Indians will also be separated in this life from many in our national communities (tribes) and from many of our relatives because they have chosen not to convert or even to return to their old

traditional belief systems. Discouraged by the dominance of White missionaries and the collusion of those missionaries with oppressive government and military subversions of Native communities and economies, many of our relatives have decided that there is no good news in the Good News and have helped to fuel this revival of the old traditions. Thus, a distance is placed between those who have become Christian and those who have as a matter of conscience decided that they cannot be Christian because Christianity represents the worst of the history of colonialism among Indian peoples in North America.

The third problem has to do with many contemporary Indian clergy. While they genuinely want the healing of Indian peoples, they find themselves caught in a quandary between the doctrinal claim of Christian exclusivity and the revival of traditional ceremonial life among Native peoples.

Yet the biblical text at hand does not necessarily read as the missionaries have insisted. Is there salvation only in Jesus? This is the way we have been conditioned to read the story in Acts, but a closer reading makes interpretation much more complex. To begin with, the use of the noun, *salvation*, and the verb, *saved*, must be read in the context of the story itself and not merely read as if the author had the usual English language meanings in mind in verse 12. The story actually begins in chapter 3 when Peter and John heal a lame man at the entrance of the Jerusalem temple. They are taken to court because they have healed him on the sabbath, the traditional day of rest for Jewish peoples on which, by divine law, no work was to be performed. Proceeding carefully, the lawyers wished to know, "By what means has this man been healed?" (Acts 4:9).

The use of the verb for healing is important because it has several meanings, including both medical healing and spiritual salvation. Indeed, it is the same verb that is translated as *saved* in verse 12. The related nouns likewise carry a range of meanings including savior and healer, salvation and healing. The question is, how have English translators moved from one meaning of the word to another in two verses with no explanation? Before we offer another translation of the text, it is important to ask how the word was first used in the story. It would seem reasonable to think that the author would have used the words in the immediate context in not terribly disparate ways.

To understand these related words in their Greek cultural context requires a reading of several hundred years of Greek literature. Already, some six hundred years before Acts was written, the Greek poet Pindar called Asclepios, the Greek god of healing, "the savior of his people." He was clearly a savior because he visited patients in his temples at night and brought to them miraculous, over-night healings of a great variety of physical maladies. There was, as yet in Greek consciousness, little attention to any notion that might be similar to the modern Christian notion of salvation. So *savior* clearly meant *healer*. Likewise, it is well-known that the word *salvation* originally referred to physical healing of an illness, and that the verb *save* referred to the action of *healing*. Luke clearly uses this meaning of the verb in the early part of this story. While Peter says to the man, "In the name of Jesus Christ of Nazareth, rise up and walk" (3:6), five verses later Luke describes the man as "the lame man who was healed" (3:11). That is to say, the lame man was saved: not for eternal life, but from his lame leg. Surely, we cannot discount the possibility that there was also a spiritual saving that happened, but that is not a part of this story. In this context salvation means physical healing.

When the priests and lawyers ask Peter and John, "By what power or by what name have you done this?" (4:7), they are asking about the physical healing. Peter's response is equally clear. The physical healing (saving) of the lame man was done by "the name of Jesus Christ of Nazareth" (4:10): "By him is this man standing before you well." This seems clearly to imply a spiritual power for physical healing (saving) that can be summoned by using the name of Jesus. And here, the name Jesus is important, because the rest of the identifying label is not name but title ("Christ") and geographical locator ("of Nazareth").

In the key verse (4:12), there is little reason to shift the meaning of the words in a wholesale fashion. Peter must be saying, "There is *healing* (not salvation) in no one else, for there is no other name under heaven given among human beings by which we must be *healed* (not saved)." While this use of language can certainly carry a double meaning, this whole story is, in fact, about a healing—the miraculous, physical healing of a lame man. To change the story to meet modern needs for salvation language does an injustice to the author and to the meaning of the story.

What can the text mean when it says there is no other name by which healing can take place? At the surface level, this claim seems ludicrous if not patently false. Even in Peter's day there were trained (however poorly by modern standards) physicians who effected healing and gave healing care to the sick. There are numerous stories from the time of Jesus that attest to the miraculous healing work of other charismatic healers in Palestine. In our American Indian communities, we have considerable experience with healing styles that use spiritual medicine and ceremony.

A survey of mission history reveals that this verse, typically used by Amer-European missionaries to coerce Indian conversion to Christianity, has been consistently misread and misinterpreted in the missionary claim of Christian exclusivity and superiority. Commentators consistently miss the most obvious point of the story, namely, that the reader is supposed to know a bit more about the name of Jesus and to draw out the meaning of the story from the meaning of the name. Like many of the particularities of ancient Palestinian culture, this is not foreign to Indian hearers of the story, since we come from cultures where names still have meaning. In the Amer-European world, however, names have largely ceased to carry any real meaning beyond euphony or family sentimentality. What do names such as Bill or Betty actually mean? Eagle Elk, Red Eagle, Bacon Rind, Earth Walker, Crazy Horse: those names can be explained. They have meaning and are carefully given to the bearers because of their meanings.

Can the meaning of the name Jesus help us to understand why Peter would insist that healing can only happen by means of this name? Few modern Christians remember that Jesus was a very common name in Palestine two millennia ago. Some will remember that it was actually a shortened form of the Hebrew Bible name of Moses' successor, Joshua. This Hebrew name was a combination of two elements, a noun and a verb, *ja* and *shua*. The noun *ja* is a shortened form of *jahweh*, one of the Hebrew names for God.[4] The verb or action part of the name (*shua*) translates "saves" or "heals". Thus the name Jesus means "God Heals (or Saves)." Here we have the meaning of the text clearly stated.

The focus, suddenly, is not on Jesus at all but on God! Jesus is not identified here as the only source of salvation or as the only savior. Rather, God is identified as the only ultimate source of healing. God is the Healer. This much every Indian person can readily acknowledge. So it has always been in our ceremonies and among our healing specialists since time immemorial. The power to heal always comes from the spiritual energy of Wakonda, even when particular individuals have been identified as the vehicles through whom certain kinds of healing or help can be facilitated.

Yet the missionaries have used this story to proclaim to us a self-serving untruth, that God has only spoken to them and only communicated through Jesus. Under the immense pressure of colonization and conquest, many of our ancestors felt they were left with little choice but to accede to the self-proclaimed superiority of the White invaders of our land; to convert to their religious belief; and to acknowledge the superiority of their God. The nature of colonization is such that it entices the strong to take advantage of the weak in all aspects of life: social, political, and economic. Such domination in the sphere of religion serves as an essential reinforcement for these other modes of domination. And so the missionaries, whose minds were every bit as much colonized as ours, saw Indian vulnerability and used that vulnerability to advance their own cause quickly and decisively.

We are not yet done, however, with the colonizer's texts. We must look at one other passage before we conclude. The beginning of the Gospel of John (1:1-4) is a wonderful, poetic statement that identifies the spiritual power that John associates with Jesus. That power, he calls *Logos*, the WORD. As this section will demonstrate, an Indian understanding of the Logos as described here springs from our own traditions and experience of the Christ as Corn Mother.

Christ, Logos, Pre-existence and Corn Mother

In the beginning was the Logos; and the Logos was with God; and the Logos was [a] God [or "divine"]. This one [*It*] was in the beginning with God. All things came into being through *It*, and nothing happened without *It*. What came into being through *It* was life; and life was the light of humanity [human beings]. And the light shines in the darkness, and the darkness cannot overcome it. (John 1:1-5)

As American Indian readers of this important colonizer sacred text, we must first come to terms with the gender of this Logos concept. It is clear from John's telling of the story that he intends us to understand a personification of the Logos, but it is certainly not clear at all that he intends us to understand it as a male personification that should thereafter be referred to as "he," which is how English translations regularly translate the pronouns of verses two to four. While the Greek noun "Logos" does indeed carry an assigned grammatical gender that is masculine, English speaking interpreters have regularly made the mistake of assuming that grammatical gender is necessarily an indication of the actual gender of the object or person to which the noun refers.

To avoid this error, we choose here to interpret the *Logos* as *It*, with a capital initial letter to indicate *Its* divine status in John's mythic construct. There is no compelling reason to interpret the Logos as male. Some Amer-European biblical interpreters have even entertained the possibility that the *Logos* is a metaphor for the Old Testament personification of *Sophia* or Wisdom as a female aspect of divinity.

The *Logos* does become manifest to humans as a male entity a few verses later (v. 14) when, implicitly, the *Logos* becomes incarnate and is identified as Jesus. How are we, then, precisely and accurately, to make the identification between Jesus and the *Logos* or between Jesus and the Christ, ultimately, since John seems to clearly infer a philosophical or theological identification between Christ and *Logos*? While this topic has been explored with considerable finesse by biblical scholars over the past century, it has a particularly promising potential for American Indian Christians in their discrete interpretation of the gospel. An interpretive space is opened if we begin with understanding a clear distinction between Jesus and the Logos (and between Jesus and the Christ), and from there attempt to define the ensuing connection between the two.

While most Amer-European Christians, especially those who are more conservative, live with a simple notion of a one-to-one equivalency of the names Jesus and Christ, a majority of theologians and biblical scholars have, especially since Rudolf Bultmann, distinguished the two both as names and as concepts, introducing, for example, the distinction between the "historical Jesus" and the "historic Christ." Bultmann found the historical Jesus to be elusive and unrecoverable, arguing that the biblical narratives were not written as or intended to be read as history. Rather, their purpose was to be generative of faith in Jesus as the Christ. Hence they were written not to convey historically accurate information, but the story and each part of it were told in ways to enhance and sustain Christian belief in the importance of Jesus as the Christ of God. Thus, Jesus becomes the human vehicle for experiencing and for communicating the more mythic, spiritual, theological, and enduring function of the Christ of God.

To apply this understanding to the Logos hymn at the beginning of the Gospel of John means that we must distinguish Jesus from the Christ of God in one very decisive way. It is clear from John 1:1-4 that the Logos, that is the Christ of God, is a pre-existent part of God. Jesus is not pre-existent in this same way. Rather, Jesus is a human being who has a birth, a beginning in time, and whose birth is identified by early Christians as a particular incarnation or manifestation of the Christ or the Logos. While Christians can claim that Jesus became the incarnation of the Christ, it would violate nearly two thousand years of European Christian history to claim that Jesus was pre-existent in the same way that the Logos is presented as pre-existing all things and participating with God even in the creation of all things. What we have said here should already signal that the two terms, Jesus and Christ, have different meanings and functions in the biblical texts, that they are not just two names for Jesus like modern American first and last names.

Up to this point, the text at hand has described the Logos as having done only two things. It was a part of creation; and some millennia later It returned to action in Its incarnation in Jesus. Yet this seems terribly limiting of God on the part of human interpreters. Why would this Logos, which was so instrumental in the creation act, have lain dormant for so much of human history? Surely there must be another way of interpreting this text.

The question of function focuses our analysis. What is it that this Logos does? How does it function as a part of God? From the little bit that we have in the Gospel of John, it seems that the Logos is some aspect of God, perhaps the creative aspect of God's self, perhaps the creative, communicative aspect of God's self as God communicates with human beings. If this is plausible, then it is unlikely that we could defend any period of inactivity or dormancy. Rather, it would seem that John merely does not mention other occurrences where the Logos or Christ was functioning in the world. Indeed, nowhere does John claim that this is the only action of the Logos since creation. Jesus, it seems, is merely one, albeit very powerful, occurrence of the Logos in human history.

This, suddenly, is a notion of Christ that Indian people can begin to understand naturally within their own cultural experiences and knowledge. If the Logos or the Christ is merely that aspect of God that communicates creativity and healing or salvation to human beings, then Indian people can contribute to Christianity's knowledge of salvation from our own experiences and memories of God's functioning among Indian communities throughout our history.

In this sense, Indians can claim to have a history of many such experiences of the Christ and can even begin to name some of them and tell the stories that go with the naming. But this also means that we can never be trapped into saying that God has only spoken this good news through Jesus, or that the only way to salvation is through a Euro-western message brought by the colonizer to the conquered.

In the final section of this chapter, we want to suggest the comparison between the mythic truths inherent in the gospel stories of Jesus and one of our American Indian traditional foundation stories.

Corn Mother as Christ

Because Indian experience of Wakonda is always a bi-gender duality, any Indian equivalent for the Euro-Christian notion of the Christ would include examples that are explicitly female. Thus, the revered mythic and historic figures of Corn Mother and White Buffalo Calf Woman, examples from two different Indian cultural traditions, would perhaps come close to functioning in ways that could be conceived of as christological. As narrative oral texts they certainly proximate the earliest Asian narratives about Jesus, and as in Christianity each of these figures continues to be significantly involved in the day-to-day well-being of the communities that tell each story. Both recount a salvific moment in the community's past, yet both continue to function to bring some element of "salvation" and wholeness to the peoples who honor the stories today.

This essay will focus on the Corn Mother narratives, which are told in a variety of versions among Indian communities of different language families, from the east coast of Canada throughout eastern North America to Florida and across the southern U.S. as far west as the Keresan Pueblos in New Mexico. The story is a part of the foundational mythic life of these different peoples, not only as an explanation for the origin of corn, but for the sacredness of life and the sacredness of food. The story involves the willing self-sacrifice (vicarious suffering) of the First Mother (Corn Mother) on behalf of her children. While initially First Man was the hunter and alone provided for the sustenance of his family, as the family grows ever larger, it became important to introduce new sources of vegetable foods. The details of the story work themselves out quite differently in different communities, with some variety in teaching emphases, but the central mythic themes are intact in all the tellings of the story.

In the Penobscot telling, the death of First Mother is actually requested by the woman herself, against the wishes of her husband, and only completed after he makes a long journey and consults with the creator himself. In a great variety of other tellings, the woman is murdered by her own children, although in each of these tellings she nevertheless willingly agrees to the killing and even invites it. In some of these stories, Corn Mother provides food in the absence of game by privately scraping or shaking the corn (and sometimes beans) off of her own body. When two of her children sneakily discover where the food is coming from, they accuse her of tricking them into cannibalism, and this becomes the excuse for the murder. In a Natchez version, two daughters accuse their mother of feeding them defecation and proceed to kill her. In another set of tellings, the murder of the woman happens as a result of the foolishness of a powerful, mythic boy child, called Blood Clot Boy, who entices the participation of his sibling. But in all these tellings the self-sacrifice of the woman is consistent and results in the enduring fecundity of the earth and production of vegetable foods.

In these stories, First Mother's death is also the first human experience of death. Her burial is accompanied by ceremony and sometimes pronounced weeping. In a common theme, the surviving family discovers that the clearing where she had been buried is miraculously filled with fully mature food plants, most prominently including corn. That is, First Mother, who is buried in the earth, becomes productive in ways that were unexpected and continues to nourish her children long after her death.

There are a number of common theological themes in these stories. The most significant is that food must henceforth be considered sacred. Eating becomes what Euro-Christian theology would signify as sacrament, because eating always involved the eating of the flesh of First Mother. She, in her dying, becomes identified with the earth, with Grandmother, *wakonda udseta*. In one telling of the story, tobacco is provided by Corn Mother in the middle of the vegetative cornucopia which grew in what had been a clearing in the forest the day before. Her voice is heard as her children approach it, announcing the import of their discovery of this surfeit of food and adding that the tobacco is to be used as a part of their prayers. It is the breath of the Mother and is to add power to their prayers as the smoke is carried up to the sky.

There is more to this story than is conveyed in the simple telling of it. Out of this story emerges a considerable theology that includes the important teaching that all life—including that life considered un-alive by Euro-science: rocks, rivers, lakes, mountains and the like—is inter-related. When one fully understands this teaching—a simple sounding notion that requires years (if not generations) of learning—one finally understands the sacramental nature of eating. Corn and all food stuffs are our relatives, just as much as those who live in adjacent lodges within our clan-cluster. Thus, eating is sacramental, to use a Euro-theological word, because we are eating our relatives. Not only are we related to corn, beans, and squash, since these things emerge immediately out of the death of Corn Mother, but even those other relatives like Buffalo, Deer, Squirrel and Fish ultimately gain their strength and growth because they too eat of the plenty provided by the Mother—eating grasses, leaves, nuts, and algae that also grow out of the

Mother's bosom. When we eat, we understand that we are benefiting from the lives that have gone before us, that all our human ancestors have also returned to the earth and have become part of what nourishes us today. Thus, one can never eat without remembering the gift of the Mother, of all our relatives in this world, and of all those who have gone before us.

Another key theological theme and a continuing cultural value among Indian peoples of different cultural affiliations is the concept of vicarious self-sacrifice. In all these stories, Corn Mother sacrifices herself willingly for the sake of her children. Accordingly, persons in our communities have lived with the notion of both ceremonial and very real physical sacrifice for the people— "that the people might live!" Ceremonially, this is lived out in Native rites like the vision quest, the sun dance, and the purification rite sometimes called "sweat lodge."

The death of Corn Mother is the first experience of death by the people. Yet this death teaches us that in terms of our day-to-day existence in Indian communities throughout North America, we understand that our ancestors continue to live in very real ways. They continue to live in a spirit world where we hope to join them at the ends of our lives here. Just as importantly, these ancestors continue to live in us, both in our memories and in our physical lives as we continue to eat the produce of the earth where they have returned in one way or another.

Finally, these stories contain some ethical/theological content, as well, focused especially toward our young men. In those variants of the story in which Corn Mother is killed by male off-spring, there in an implicit warning to men about the potential for male violence in society. Men are to pay attention to the results of immature male decision-making, especially when it leaves women out of the decision-making process. We are particularly to be attentive to the potential for inherent male strength to explode in foolish, unpredictable and irreparable ways against women. Moreover, we are to pay attention to the inherent valuing of female gifts and wisdom in our communities. We are to forever remember that healing in the form of both food and spiritual sustenance have come to us traditionally not through men but through a woman, whether it is White Buffalo Woman or Corn Mother. This wisdom provides constant temperance of male dominance, aggression and assertiveness in our communities.

Conclusion

The story of Corn Mother is one example of the power and cosmic balancing of American Indian mythic traditions. Why should Indian people be coerced to give up God's unique self-disclosure to us? Why ought Indian people learn to identify after the fact with God's self-disclosure to some other people in a different place and time in a mythic tradition that is culturally strange and alienating? Our traditions are ancient and precious and are to be revered and lived. To the modern Indian traditionalist, there is little need to pay any heed to the colonizer's churches or doctrines.

On the other hand, many who have been converted to those churches may also find these ancient traditions to be precious. Indian Christians will want to struggle in the coming generation to understand their Christian commitments increasingly on their own terms in ways that incorporate their own cultural traditions of the sacred. The Christian Indian interpretation of Jesus as the Christ will eventually differ considerably from the interpretation offered in the colonizer churches and hierarchies. This process of nativizing Indian Christianity already began with the first Indian ministers in the seventeenth century and continues in the bold and energetic work of a few modern Indian ministers.

In terms of an emergent communal vision of healing for a people that have been long abused and marginalized by the colonial relationships in North America, Indian people are increasingly making the former choice. They are insisting that the relationship between Indian peoples and the churches is so fractured as to be irreconcilable from the vantage point of American Indian liberation. The spiritual hope today for Indian nations, they argue, is to recover their historical and traditional ceremonial forms. A great many Indian families have been evangelized into the churches, of course, and the churches will continue to be some force in every Indian community. Yet, those congregations and missions have long ceased to grow and are in decline these days. The younger members of churched families have tended to be among those who have made the transition back to traditional ceremonies and religious traditions.

The colonizer churches themselves will necessarily have to rethink their notion of Christian exclusivity and make room for American Indian religious traditions as being potentially as powerful and salvific as the best vision well-intentioned peoples have for Christianity. This interpretation of two important texts may make it possible to understand the notion of Christ with much greater inclusivity and parity of power between colonizer and colonized. Likewise, it should be possible today for a mutual respect to emerge that will allow Christians to acknowledge the inherent spiritual power and goodness of American Indian religious traditions.

origin, purpose, destiny of humankind

doctrine of humanity / Humans and their relationship to God

CHAPTER 5

THEOLOGICAL ANTHROPOLOGY

Is the Windingo Real?

> *The Berens River Indian is responding to a real danger when he flees from a cannibal monster or murders a human being who is turning into a windigo.... To act or feel otherwise would stamp an individual either as a fool or as a phenomenal example of intellectual emancipation.*
>
> A. Irving Hallowell[1]

What is the nature of humanity? And what is religion? These profound questions have informed the academic discipline of anthropology, while Native people have lived their lives, carried out their ceremonies, and generally been who they will be. The heart of religious inquiry for Christians has been the question, What sets human beings apart as special creations of God? while the subject of scientific inquiry for anthropologists has been, What constitutes the common essence of humanity? The basic issues in this chapter are the definitions of humanity and culture.

Theological anthropology is concerned with defining the human person as a religious being. For Native Americans,

 paper

their intimate relationship with the natural environment blurs the distinctions between human and non-human. Human beings are not the only people in the world. The world is populated with a large number of persons, human and non-human, whose interactions constitute the Native world. We must move beyond the Christian tradition of humans as unique creations of God to the idea that the world of persons is all embracing.[2] Native people believe that they share the world with spiritual beings with whom they must establish relationships.

Christianity, on the other hand, begins with the belief that human beings are the ultimate creation of God. The sin of Adam and Eve, however, complicates the understanding of humanity. How could a God who was all good create imperfect humans?

A Brief History of Anthropology

The academic discipline of anthropology emerged in the late nineteenth century as an attempt to find universal principles of human culture, and in America, its primary object of study has been American Indian tribes. Lewis Henry Morgan is generally considered the father of American anthropology with his systematic study of kinship systems.[3] Morgan's studies of kinship and house types established the systematic study of American Indian cultures.

Anthropologists seek to define the essence of culture. Definitions of culture have ranged from Clark Wissler's materialist approach of listing physical objects as culture traits[4] to Clifford Geertz's semiotic "webs of meaning."[5] Anthropologists, however, proceed from an etic viewpoint, the outsider looking into a culture in search of some generalizable premise. The Native proceeds from the emic viewpoint, explaining custom, behavior, and belief from his or her own belief system. The anthropologist attempts to understand the Native viewpoint while maintaining the scientific objectivity to assess its content in terms of generalizable principles of human behavior. This generalizability is the keystone of anthropology as science, because it allows people to predict the outcome of events. If there is a basic unity in the human psyche, then the behavior of individuals in similar circumstances is predictable. This scientific approach is, however, itself a product of a particular time and culture—seventeenth-century western Europe. It represents the culmination of intellectual traditions originating with the Greeks, the Romans, Judaism, Christianity, and the fourteenth-century renaissance in Europe. The notions of skepticism, natural law, and universal truth derived from particular cultural values and historical circumstances.

Science is, at its heart, a set of assumptions about the world. The belief in the uniformity of human nature is just that, a belief. Aristotelean logic shows us the distinction between validity and truth. An argument may be valid if it follows the rules, but if its premises are false, its conclusion cannot be true. One can prove logically that the moon is made of green cheese, but this conclusion flies in the face of empirical evidence to the contrary. Assumptions about the nature of religious experience can never be proven as fact. Attempts to generalize about religion are exercises in fitting the data to the theory.

The nature of Indian languages indicates a basic philosophical distinction between the scientific stance of anthropology and the epistemology of Native peoples. Indian languages have markers that distinguish between knowledge that an individual has from personal experience and that which is heard from other people.[6] Gladys Reichard in her study of Navajo chants said that none of her "informants" would attempt a synthesis of the system such as she carried out. Each was a specialist in his field of knowledge and knew what he had studied, but would not presume to speak about other people's knowledge.[7]

Clifford Geertz distinguishes between local knowledge and global knowledge. This formulation pinpoints the distinction between western science and theology, which assumes to define knowledge that is absolute and available to all people, and knowledge in native communities, which is personal. This statement is indeed a generalization of the sort that anthropologists make, and it points to the problem of translating one system of knowledge into another.[8]

Robert Lowie described religious experience as unknowable.[9] Anthony F. C. Wallace categorized religions into thirteen practices and four general categories.[10] Studies of Indian religions in the early twentieth century subscribed to the principle of cultural diffusion and looked for the origins of religious practices. Leslie Spier studied and categorized examples of the Plains Sun Dance.[11] Ruth Benedict developed categories of visionary and shamanistic practices on the Plains and, in *Patterns of Culture*, proposed behavioral categories of Dionysian, Apollonian, and Megalomaniac for the Plains, Pueblo, and Northwest Coast cultures.[12] Elsie Clews Parsons offered a general categorization of Pueblo religious practices.[13] Other scholars sought causal explanations for major phenomena. Åke Hultkrantz postulated that dreams and visionary experiences are the source of a concept of the soul and explained them as evidence of life after death.[14] It is, however, that emotional experience of anxiety, fear, and wonder in the face of the power of the environment that best characterized the religious experiences of many Indian people. The important point is that human beings realize their humanity in relationship to the beings in nature—trees, rocks, water, winds, animals—anything that has the capacity to move and change.

The Concept of Personhood

The Windigo is a gigantic cannibal spirit who inhabits the woods in northern Minnesota. It is hairy, it has a long, sharp toenail on its right foot, and it has a heart of ice. The lone hunter who encounters the Windigo is seized with its spirit and may begin to kill and consume his relatives. Recorded instances of cannibalism in Minnesota in the late nineteenth century attest to the power of the Windigo. Although it may be seen as a metaphor for the cold, hunger, and fear that the Chippewa hunter experienced in the harshness of a Minnesota winter, it is also, however, very real in terms of the understanding and emotions of that individual.

Language is the key to world view, and linguistic studies demonstrate those relationships of knowledge and power.[15] A. Irving Hallowell, an anthropologist studying the Ojibwa in Canada, noticed that the language had markers for animate and inanimate categories, but these were much different from English categories. Hallowell, searching for a generalizable principle to explain the distinctions, asked the man "Are all the stones we see around us alive?" The man thought for a while and replied, "No, but *some* are."[16] It is the *some* that constitute the manifestation of power that characterizes Indian ways of thinking about personhood.

Iroquois people in upstate New York believed that souls were capable of leaving their bodies and roaming at will. Human souls could enter the bodies of animals, and vice versa.[17] Mutability is the essence of personhood, and it is evidence of the nature of spiritual power. An important aspect of spiritual power was the ability of a spiritual being to change its form. Humans who acquired spiritual power might change their forms to those of animals. Among the Ojibwa, a person initiated into the second degree of the Midewiwin could assume the form of any animal; particularly might he or she assume the form of the animal associated with the specific degree, which might depend on the community in which the ceremony took place.[18] Mutability of form blurs the boundaries of self and non-self by allowing individuals to transcend those boundaries at will when they acquire spiritual power.

The Nature of Power

A person walks along a path in the forest, and suddenly, a rock bounces down the hill, hitting the person on the head. Why? "Power is thought of only when it manifests itself in some very striking way."[19] Power is immanent, manifest in the environment. Orenda, Manitou, and Wakan are expressions of this immanent power for the Iroquois, Algonquian, and Siouian people respectively. Power is evident in all things that exhibit the capacities of will and volition. The notion of power also captures the strongly emotional basis for Indian religious belief, an element often missing in the descriptions of human behavior that characterize early ethnographic studies of Indian societies. The concept of power is the most fruitful of anthropological approaches to the study of American Indian religions.

The idea of power has become an important intellectual concept in academic circles in recent time. Michel Foucault explicates the relationship between knowledge and power.[20] Post-modernism, post-colonialism, and post-structuralism have focused on power relationships in the creation and dissemination of knowledge. Anthropologists studying Indian religions describe power as a function of relationships. It allows individuals to influence the behavior of other people to obtain their wants—physical, material, and emotional. In the religious world (here defining religion as a system of relationships between the human and the spiritual world), people can gain knowledge from spiritual beings that allows them to affect the world. People with certain kinds of knowledge can cure illness; others can control weather, or predict where animals will be found for hunting, or find lost objects.

Power is manifest in the unusual, things that behave in unexpected ways. Where science seeks the generalizable, power resides in difference. Mircea Eliade described the notion of the sacred as follows: "It is important to bring out this notion of peculiarity conferred by an unusual or abnormal experience, for, properly considered, singularization as such depends upon the very dialectic of the sacred. The most elementary hierophanies, that is, are nothing but a radical ontological separation of some object from the surrounding cosmic zone; some tree, some stone, some place, by the mere fact that it reveals that it is sacred, that it has been, as it were, 'chosen' as the receptacle for a manifestation of the sacred, is thereby ontologically separated from all other stones, trees, places, and occupies a different, a supernatural plane."[21]

secret / inner teachings

Power depends on secrecy. It is esoteric. The academic world looks at knowledge as public, available to all, because it is generalizable to all. The intellectual challenge is to analyze the ways in which knowledge is created, disseminated, and utilized, in order to understand the implications of its use as a source of power. Those who violate it are subject to sanction. Washington Matthews, a military man assigned to the Indian agency on the Navajo reservation, observed and recorded a number of Navajo curing ceremonies, called "chants." During the course of recording the Night Chant, a ceremony lasting nine nights, Matthews suffered a stroke that left him partially paralyzed. Some of the Navajo people attending the ceremony attributed the stroke to the fact that he did not know about the ceremony and was overwhelmed by its power.[22]

Anthropological studies of witchcraft provide numerous examples of belief systems in native cultures analogous to but certainly not identical with evil in Christianity. Witchcraft is defined as the use of personal power to control the behavior of other people.[23] It is based on the idea that each individual has power to control other beings, human or spiritual. Those who use their power to control other humans are evil in the Indian sense.

Sacred Clowns

The structuralist anthropology of Claude Lévi-Strauss postulates that binary oppositions in meaning are essential to exchange of goods and services in society. Using the notion of totems, relationships between humans and the spiritual world—plants, animals, things that demonstrate power— Lévi-Strauss maintains that seemingly disparate meanings can relate to each other.[24] Categories of beings, however, differ significantly among cultural groups.

Anthropological studies of sacred clowns focus on their inversion of the meaning of the world.[25] Clowns eat feces, drink urine, and perform sexual acts in public. They try to build

structures of ashes, as Don Talayesva describes in his account
of participation in a clowning performance.[26] The clowns are
sacred because they represent the ability to deal with the chaos
of uncontrolled power that threatens social order.

The sacred is the unexpected, and humor is the juxtaposi-
tion of things that we don't expect. Eliade's definition of the
sacred in terms of its "peculiarity" shows us how it is possible
for *some* stones to be alive. The peculiarity of the clown's world
is to turn reality on its head, to do the unexpected in order to
provoke laughter at their foolishness but at the same time to
emphasize the fact that for a time they stand outside the accepted order of society, and because of that they are powerful.

Humor in the context of sacred clowns, contraries, heyokas,
and other ritualized behavior, is the reversal of meaning that
makes people laugh at the bizarre, the unusual, or the unexpected. Black Elk describes the role of the Heyoka, who per-
forms ordinary actions in reverse (riding backwards on his
horse, saying goodby when he means hello, for instance) as in-
spiring laughter and thus opening the minds of individuals to
the voices of the spirits. As Black Elk commented, "You have
noticed that truth comes into this world with two faces. One is
sad with suffering, and the other laughs, but it is the same
face."[27] The power of the clowns is to reveal the ambiguity of
the world.[28] When Don Talayesva instructed his fellow clowns
to bring logs and they brought ashes, the ludicrousness of their
activities brings laughter, but it also reinforces the idea of what
proper behavior ought to be.

Myth and Sacred Text

The cosmologies of Native people explain their relationship
with the forces of nature and with each other. Although missionaries generally dismissed origin traditions as made-up stories, Franz Boas found the basis for understanding common
humanity in collections of oral traditions and the study of language. Creation stories account for aspects of the present

world. A Seneca origin tradition tells of a woman who lived with her husband and sons in the sky world above. One day she heard someone whispering in her ear, but no one was there. When it became apparent that she was pregnant, her husband accused her of having a lover. He ordered his sons to pull up the great tree that stood in the center of the world, and he pushed the woman through the hole thus created. She tried to cling to the earth, and dirt and seeds lodged under her fingernails, but she lost her grip and fell toward the water below the sky world. The birds, however, flew under her and took her on their backs. They could not support her for long, but a turtle rose from the water, and the birds set her down on its back. The turtle's shell expanded, and it became the earth upon which the Seneca live today. The seeds and dirt lodged under her fingernails became the source of plants on the earth. When her twin sons were born, one emerged naturally, but the other tore his way through her side, killing her in the process. They then proceeded to shape the earth, the good twin creating things useful and helpful to humans, the evil twin creating things that were harmful.[29]

Lakota history begins with the story of White Buffalo Calf Woman. Two hunters encountered a beautiful young woman on the prairie. One looked at her with lust, but as he approached her, a cloud descended and engulfed him, and when it lifted he was a maggot-ridden corpse. The other approached her with respect, and she taught him the ceremonies that the tribe would perform to assure that the buffalo would allow themselves to be killed. She then transformed herself into a white buffalo calf and ran away across the prairie.[30]

The origin stories reveal both the similarities and the distinctions between Christian and American Indian traditions. In the Christian tradition, God is omniscient, omnipotent, and omnipresent. In Native American traditions, power is immanent in natural forces. In the Christian tradition, God, in the person of Jesus, is concerned with the salvation of individuals. In Native American traditions, deities are teachers and protectors.

Sacred Time and Sacred Space

Anthropology has taken a synchronic view of culture—freezing Natives in time and assigning to them the status of "Other" that makes them objects of study.[31] Linguistics as a branch of anthropological inquiry has, however, offered insights into Native world views and systems of knowledge. The relationship between language and human behavior has been a matter of on-going debate in the academic world.

The work of Benjamin Whorf is important as a source of understanding of Native world views. He described the Hopi language as concerned with anticipation and manifestation of the heart. The Hopi believe that the heart is the source of emotion and intellect (English terms that do not do full justice to the complexity of these concepts). Hoping, wishing, desiring and expecting—all are aspects of the heart, and what comes to pass in human life is a result of the heart. The sense of time for the Hopi is not divided linguistically into the categories of past, present, and future as in English. Everything that exists has manifested itself and constitutes what the English language might express as the past. That which is anticipated constitutes the future.[32] Anticipation for a people whose lifestyle is based in subsistence agriculture means that they expect that events that happened in the past will repeat themselves, and they do. What happened in the past will happen again in the future, and thus the distinctions of time in the English language have little meaning to the Hopi.

The Mayan civilization in Mesoamerica developed a very sophisticated system of time keeping and a hierarchy of leaders whose terms of office were governed by various cyclical patterns of celestial events. "Within each community, municipal authority rotated among the territorial divisions, and presumably their principal lineages, on a four-year cycle." This system provided for an equitable distribution of power that helped to avoid conflict and disorder.[33]

Because people feel that they are a part of the natural environment, and because they can establish relationships with natural forces, they also feel that their activities are essential to the cycles of nature. The input of human energy into the environment through ceremony is more important than the physical activities of hunting, gathering, and cultivating. The ceremonies are essential to assure that the anticipated events of the world manifest themselves. By remembering the past, the Hopi anticipate the future, and because they are causal agents, they create the future.

Indian cultures evolved in harmony with nature. Bennett described subsistence economies as the first solar-powered societies. People are mainly concerned with what reoccurs because they depend upon plants and animals. Thinking about the future corresponds with the repetition of events, hence human thought becomes a causative agent in the processes of the world. Ceremony, the input of human energy into the environment, is essential for the continuation of the world.

Models of Cultural Change

Anthropologists have played an important role as experts whose opinions were valued by government officials making policy that affected American Indians in the late nineteenth and early twentieth century. Accounts of the historical experience of Indians were premised on various ideas of cultural evolution and racial superiority that grew out of studies following the scientific model. Craniology and phrenology, based in the work of Samuel Morris in the 1830's postulated that intellectual capacity, based on brain size, could be used to rank humans from superior to inferior.[34]

Anthropologists have been concerned in a historical sense with the impact of cultures on each other. In the early twentieth century the construct of the vanishing native inspired anthropologists to capture what they could of what they perceived as the vestiges of primal American Indian cultures. The impact of colonialism and technology on Native peoples worldwide was perceived as threatening the pristine nature of cultures from whom data could be acquired.

Anthropologists turned to the task of defining acculturation as the way in which one culture displaced another.[35] The process was described as the replacement of the values of a subordinate culture with those of a dominant one. This formulation represents an assumption of the scientific paradigm of anthropology, that there are universal truths of culture and that evolution of culture is an absolute. Historically, the replacement of Indian religion with Christianity was a primary objective of federal policy in an attempt to integrate American Indians into American society.

The disciplines of anthropology and theology are, however, themselves cultures, with their own rules, conventions, assumptions, and kinship structure in the roles of faculty and students. They evolve, and as do all dynamic systems of human interaction, their intellectual constructs change. The discipline of anthropology has evolved to recognize that the concept of culture, in a rapidly changing world system of economic interdependency and information exchange, is not a static entity. It is increasingly difficult to say that a set of cultural values can be so specifically defined that its total replacement by another set of values can be observed.

This formulation is an acknowledgment of the historical dimensions of the evolution of anthropology as an academic discipline. The study of culture involves the observer, but it also involves larger historical and societal forces. Anthropologists can find few pristine societies to study. Culture is a moving target, not a static entity.

Anthony F. C. Wallace analyzed the phenomenon of revitalization in Indian cultures. He formulated a model in which rejection of foreign culture leads to renewed, but changed, culture. His study of the Handsome Lake religion among the Seneca demonstrated how a tribal community could rely on men who had experienced visionary experiences to institute new ways of knowing about the world.[36] Early revitalization movements were generally reported to involve total rejection of new cultural elements. Neolin, a Delaware prophet who gained attention in 1763 and whose teachings inspired the Ottawa leader Pontiac, called for rejection of the white man's customs. The Delaware's culture had been significantly changed by contact with Christianity, but Neolin interpreted Christian elements in a traditional way to persuade his followers to change their ways.[37]

The Ghost Dance in the late nineteenth century integrated elements of older ceremonies with a new philosophy of peaceful resistance to white colonization. Ghost Dancers believed that their ceremonies would cause the world to be renewed with the return of dead ancestors and the buffalo and for some tribes, the complete destruction of white people.[38] The Bola Maru in California, which persisted among the Kashiya Pomo in Northern California until the 1950's, was a continuation of an earlier Ghost Dance movement that started in about 1870.[39]

Although some scholars still follow acculturation models, more are accepting models of syncretism (elements of one culture become part of another). From the perspective of Christianity, syncretism represents a contamination of truth. From a Native perspective, it represents a way of assimilating new cultural elements into existing systems, and although it is certainly a form of cultural change, it is accommodation rather than acculturation.

Alfonso Ortiz, a member of San Juan Pueblo and an anthropologist, once described the visit of Jesse Jackson, then a candidate for the presidency of the United States, to the Hopi tribe. Jackson was attempting to enlist the support of the Hopi to his Rainbow Coalition of ethnic groups who would elect him to office. His speech was delivered in his characteristic rhythm and cadence, with rhyme and emotion. The Hopi listened politely, and Jackson departed. Shortly thereafter, the Hopi held one of their ceremonies, and a clown appeared dressed in a blue, pin stripe suit, with an orange Afro wig, and proceeded to replicate Jackson's speech in Hopi. Ortiz described the event as a typically Pueblo way of dealing with new influences. As he said, if the clown became a permanent part of future Hopi ceremonies, it would mean that Jackson was an influence on the culture. If not, the Hopi had dismissed him.[40]

Syncretism as a model of cultural change is particularly evident in many of the ceremonies of the Pueblos in the south-west. The often forcible and violent suppression of native religions by Spanish priests beginning in 1598, revolt in 1680, and Spanish military subjugation in 1692 created a system of power and resistance that shaped contemporary Pueblo religious expression. Pueblo people have adopted forms of Catholic observance and belief, and statues of Catholic saints are carried in ceremonies observing their name days, but these events are part of the ceremonial cycle that carries the events of the natural year forward in ways that promote the subsistence cycle. Syncretism thus incorporates religious elements of Catholicism with Native practices in an efficacious way.[41]

The idea of inculturation as a model stems from a theological notion that Christ is absolute and all cultures demonstrate his presence but must be made to realize it. From an anthropological viewpoint, the idea of inculturation (a particularly Catholic concept) is an aspect of the absolutist stance of anthropology. Religion and science are thus aspects of a notion of absolute truth. All things are knowable, and all stem from a single origin.[42]

Indian Anthropologists

Indians as anthropologists occupy an ambiguous status. As participants in the academic world they are expected to maintain the stance of objectivity that the discipline demands. But as members of tribes and participants in the activities of their communities, they are part of the study. Because they are trained as observers and recorders, however, they bring special skills to the recording of knowledge. Alfonso Ortiz is probably the most widely known Indian anthropologist who was able to bridge the academic and tribal world successfully, and even he was criticized in his home pueblo of San Juan for revealing information that should remain secret.

Cast in the role of the "informant," Indian people shared knowledge with anthropologists, sometimes in exchange for money, sometimes because they feared the loss of knowledge because younger generations were no longer interested in or capable of understanding it. Plenty-Coups revealed the secret of his great vision because he wanted to assure the continuance of the Crow people.[43] George Hunt collected priceless materials from Kwakiutl households, which had a strong tradition of private ownership of such property, and sold it to Franz Boas, who established the anthropology department at Columbia University in the early twentieth century.[44] Francis LaFlesche provided sacred artifacts and knowledge of secret societies and ceremonials of the Omaha to Alice Fletcher.[45] In the course of these activities, such individuals received informal training in anthropological and ethnographic field methods.

They also represent, however, one of the main methodological dilemmas of early anthropology. Those people willing to participate in the gathering of information were often unusual in their own societies—products of white fathers and Indian mothers (Hunt), members of highly prestigious families (LaFlesche), or leaders in their own right (Plenty-Coups). To what extent could their experiences serve as representative of social values in the social group as a whole?

In contemporary American society, Vine Deloria, Jr. (Standing Rock Sioux author and activist) wrote:

> Into each life, it is said, some rain must fall. Some people have bad horoscopes, others take tips on the stock market. McNamara created the TRX and the Edsel. But Indians have been cursed above all other people. Indians have anthropologists.[46]

The irony is that in many societies, contemporary Indian people are turning to the knowledge recorded by anthropologists to recover in some way the traditions that were suppressed by federal policy, lost in the boarding school experience, and condemned by Christian missionaries. However problematic the relationship between Indians and anthropologists, it seems that their very presence has been subsumed as a factor in the lives of Indian people today.

CHAPTER 6

SIN AND ETHICS

The Notion of Sin

I feel that I am a sinner and every thing that I do is displeasing to God. I wish that the missionaries would pray for me in case I die and go to hell and be tormented forever.
John Long, Choctaw Nation
a student at Elliot Mission, 1821[1]

The crux of Christian conversion for Indian people is the idea of sin, and particularly the idea of original sin. Indians must accept the idea of sinfulness and the saving grace of Christ's crucifixion to be Christian. But this subjection to the will of an omniscient, omnipresent God whose omnipotence determines human fate is very much at odds with traditional Indian ways of seeking spiritual power through direct communication with spiritual forces. Dreams, vision quests, and initiation rites give Indians access to spiritual power. The concepts of sin and of a singular, omnipotent God are quite foreign to traditional Indian beliefs.

The difficulty of imposing the Christian notion of sin upon Indian people is apparent in the native words that missionaries have used to try to convey the meaning of sin. These words generally mean to make a mistake, or to be lost, which implies non-willful behavior. Harry Long, a Methodist minister and member of the Mvscogee (Creek) Nation of Oklahoma, said that in the Creek language the word means "to bother someone," a phrase implying an interference with the will of another person. For the Navajo, wrong acts do not constitute willful disobedience to laws but the result of not knowing what one is doing.[2] This idea is not alien to Christianity. The Greek term *hamartia*, which is translated as sin, is also an archery term meaning literally to miss the mark with one's arrow.[3]

The Choctaw words glossed as sin by Cyrus Byington, a missionary from the American Board of Commissioners for Foreign Missions in the early nineteenth century, were *aiashachi* and *aiyoshoba*. His English gloss of *Aiashachi* is, however, "to err at; to make a mistake at, or by means of; to sin about, or at, to overlook," and *aiyoshoba* is a noun meaning "error, wandering; sin; place of sin." The root *yoshoba* is glossed first as "lost; out of the way, gone astray" and only then as "sinful, evil, wicked, guilty, ill; immoral; iniquitous; reprobate; vicious, wanton."[4] One contemporary Choctaw speaker gave the primary meaning of *yoshoba* as wandering in the wilderness, as wild animals do (the connection to *nashoba*, wolf, indicates the primacy of this meaning).[5] These terms hardly equate with Christian ideas of depravity and original sin.

Will and Power

The nature of human will is one of the most profound questions in Christian theology. Are humans totally subject to the will of a supreme God, or do they have freedom of choice? In Christian doctrine, the choice of Adam and Eve to eat of the fruit of the tree of knowledge in the Garden of Eden led to the fall of humanity. But having made the choice, their subsequent banishment from the Garden made them subject to God's punishment. It also, however, led them to a sense of self-awareness which made them fully human. No longer blessed with innocence, they became aware of their nakedness and the nature of good and evil. In early Puritan thought, human life became the working out of God's will on Earth, and natural order was the result of God's creative force. Indians represented wilderness, the disruption of natural order, and ultimately, agents of the Devil, who challenged God's will.[6]

Indian beliefs, posited in the idea of immanent power, see the forces of the natural environment as beings possessing will and volition. Human will finds its analogy in the unpredictable behavior of natural forces such as wind and running water. Will is the main motivation for human action in Indian societies. There are two aspects of will. In the more philosophical sense, it is the operation of human action in the on-going relationship between humans and spiritual beings. Maintaining the appropriate relationship through daily behavior and ceremonial action is essential to the continuation of the world. Thus the Hopi see the future as the coming into reality of their wishes, and the Cherokee renew their world every year with the Green Corn Ceremony.[7]

Will in the social sense is the matter of choice among options, as in the story of Adam and Eve. The Christian notions of good and evil are based on obedience or disobedience to the laws of God. In Indian societies, the idea of evil is associated with the term witchcraft, which can be defined as an individual's ability to exert control over the actions of another person and deprive him or her of freedom of action. One form of witchcraft is the use of love medicine—charms, incantations, manipulation of objects, to make someone love or fall out of love with someone.[8] The power of romantic love, an intense emotion, both deprives someone of will and makes him or her susceptible to control by another (the idea of seduction). Black Elk referred to it as a kind of sickness.[9]

Will can involve decisions to use power gained from a relationship with a spirit in either beneficial or destructive ways. Because of constraints of secrecy in initiation rites and the ineffable nature of visionary experiences, the true power of an individual is unknowable to others. It is known only by its manifestations in human behavior and its results. Hence, individuals whose actions are perceived as particularly powerful may be held in reverence, but also in awe, or regarded with some fear.[10] Those who choose to use power to affect other human beings for their own self-interest, i.e., love medicine, causing harm to others, are considered evil. Historically documented cases of the killing of individuals suspected of this kind of behavior demonstrate the power of this belief system.[11]

Sin and Sexuality

St. Augustine equated human sexuality with original sin. In the act of intercourse, humans passed the taint of sin to their children.[12] Augustine's *Confessions* was the work of a man plagued by his own sexual urges, which strongly influenced his attitude toward sex as a sinful act. The attitudes toward sex in American Indian societies were generally forgiving for men, while chastity was a highly valued quality for women. In the Oglala Lakota Sun Dance, young unmarried women who wished to serve as attendants to the male dancers had to make a public declaration of their virginity.[13] Cheyenne women were noted for their chastity among other northern Plains tribes.[14] Sex as inappropriate behavior occurred in the form of adultery. For plains tribes, unfaithful wives were punished by husbands by having their noses cut off, or being subjected to gang rape by her husband's comrades. A similar occasion of rape was recorded among the Cherokee by James Adair in the mid-eighteenth century.[15]

Sex was not a source of sin but of social order in tribal societies where kinship was the organizing principle. Matrilineal and patrilineal descent patterns influenced attitudes toward sex. In European society, patrilineal societies tended to emphasize female chastity in order to assure the paternity of their children. In Native American societies, it is dangerous to generalize across the diversity of social structures, but where men as hunters contributed the greatest amount of the food supply, societies tended to be patrilineal, and women's chastity and fidelity were highly val-

ued. In agriculturally based societies, women generally are responsible for the majority of food production, for maintaining
the houses in settled villages, and afford latitude to men who are
always outsiders to their wives' families. Kinship structures such
as clans and moieties provide greater structure in social organization and ceremonial cycles than in the more fluid and family-
based organization of hunter tribes.[16]

Abstinence from sex was often an aspect of the purification
that preceded participation in ceremonial activity. The purification process often included sweat bathing. The ultimate intent
was to remove the aura of human life that marked men as different from spirits or from animals who were their prey.[17] As Don
Talayesva, a Hopi man whose life history was recorded in the
1930's, remarked of his activities before a Katcina dance, "During the practice nights I stayed away from love-making because I
wanted to keep a good name and never start a rumor, 'Talayesva
sleeps with the girls while he practices for the dance.'"[18]

Sexual behavior has ethical implications because the birth of
children represents responsibility to community. The defining
aspect of women's roles comes in their ability to bear children.
The Navajo story of the separation of the sexes illuminates the
complementary roles of men and women in Navajo society
that necessitated marriage and childrearing as the main function of sex. In one version of the story, the wife of a chief committed adultery on the banks of the river that flowed through
Navajo territory, and when her husband observed the act, he
struck her. This act led the woman's mother to take her daughter and the other women away. They declared that they did not
need the men, and they built rafts and crossed the river to the
other side. When it became apparent that the women were not
going to return, the men began to cook and till the fields. The
pregnant women gave birth to children during the first
months of the separation, but the fields that they tried to establish were not fertile. They had little to eat, and no prospect of
sexual satisfaction, and they began to masturbate with animals
and wild roots and other things. They began to give birth to
strange, deformed creatures. Finally, in desperation, they went

to the riverbank and called to the men to take them back, which they did. The moral of the story is that men and women belong together, and that their union is necessary for the happiness and harmony of the Navajo people.[19]

Although sex has a definite purpose in life in terms of procreation, that is not its sole purpose. Talayesva's openness about his love affairs indicates an enjoyment of sexual pleasure. The Navajo squaw dance allows young women to choose young men as their partners. The preliminaries of the Lakota Sun Dance includes a day during which sexual license is granted to encourage the increase of the buffalo.

Death and Afterlife

When the sense of power is immanent, the idea of an afterlife is less important than it is when power is remote. Although the stereotype of a "Happy Hunting Ground" is well established, the continuation of personal existence after death has less importance in tribal societies than in Christianity. The concept of hell and punishment in an afterlife is documented in ethnographic accounts. A Choctaw account was that after death the soul of the individual traveled to another world. They had to cross over a bridge over a river. Those who had led good lives crossed into the world where deer were plentiful and the climate always mild. Those who had led bad lives fell off the bridge into whirlpools filled with toads and lizards and snakes, and were perpetually hungry.[20] *Hell*

At San Juan Pueblo, the ceremony surrounding death transcended the dual social structure of the society, the Summer and Winter moieties, and brought the community together to mark the passage of the individual to the world of spirits from which all people had emerged. All would return to that world. Those who had led good lives were buried with a handful of cornmeal under the arm as sustenance for the journey. Those who had led bad lives were buried with several handfuls of cornmeal because the journey would be longer.[21]

What is good? The answer in Indian communities lies in the responsibility to kin and the community. Spirituality is a way of gaining access to power that can then be used for the good of one's relatives and the rest of the community. Kinship defines the appropriate roles that people play in relation to other people and the responsibilities that they have toward them. In matrilineal societies, the mother's brother has a special responsibility to see to the training of her male children and especially their training for ceremonial duties.

Appropriate behavior is the basis for ethical behavior. What is important in Indian communities is the integrity of the individual. Western European society glorifies individuality. While Indian communities respect the integrity of the individual, they expect the individual to exercise the responsibility to act according to the expectations of family and community. Ella Deloria noted that for the Lakota the worst thing that could be said of an individual was that he or she acted "as if they had no relatives."

The maintenance of appropriate social relationships is essential to good behavior. These relationships are not only human ones but those with the other-than-human persons who live in the natural world and whose presence constitutes the spiritual world. God is called upon as grandfather, thus developing a sense of the importance of intergenerational relationships. The relationship among different generations is exemplified in the idea that the present is actually 200 years long. An individual can look back to past generations and forward to future generations in a way that spans at least 200 years of consciousness. Respect for the elderly and reliance upon their wisdom is acknowledgment of their roles as repositories of knowledge upon which younger generations can draw.

Sin and Law

In Indian communities, deities do not hand down laws for human behavior. Origin stories may contain models of appropriate and inappropriate behavior. Strikingly for the Navajos, the elaborate origin stories that undergird the ceremonial chants demonstrate what happens when people indulge in things they have been told not to do. The result is usually physical illness, and even death, which is rectified by some spiritual power. Thus, the Mountainway Chant tells of a young woman who slept with a handsome young man after a dance. When she woke in the morning her handsome husband was a Bear, and he pursued her over mountains, and through rocky terrain that bruised her feet. When she finally reached her family, she was restored with a sweat bath.[22]

In Christianity, the fall of humanity was absolute, and the single redemptive act was the sacrifice of Jesus Christ. The power of ceremony in Indian society is that it gives human beings the power to renew their worlds on a regular basis. Because deity is immanent power, humans interact with powers in an ongoing fashion, and ceremonies have the ability to restore the world to a state of initial perfection.

Sin and Sickness

In the story of Job, physical affliction is a sign of God's will, not as a form of punishment, but as a test of Job's devotion. Sickness as punishment for sin is, however, widely accepted as a sign of evil in the world, and as punishment for the depravity of human beings. The sources of sickness in Native societies are either the malevolent actions of other people with the power to affect one's well being, or contact with spiritual forces whose power one does not understand or which is greater than one's own. This contact often takes place when the individual is outside the confines of the village or social group because the wilderness is the realm of spiritual forces. What human beings have not organized in their social and physical spaces in which they live is potentially harmful.

Sickness can be defined as a state of disharmony or imbalance, either in the physical processes of the human body or in the social balance that keeps the community functioning smoothly. It is characterized by disorientation, physical pain and dis-ease, and/or inappropriate behavior (generally excessive behavior, such as excessive anxiety, sexual behavior, or mania). It may result from willfully inappropriate behavior that brings individuals into contact with spirits, and thus it may be analogous to the Christian concept of punishment.

Healing is an important role of powerful individuals who have the knowledge to deal with spiritual powers. The restoration of an appropriate balance of powers results in a cure.

Ethical Values and the Concept of Sin

The concept of sin in Christianity depends upon the concept of a supreme being who created a perfect world peopled by imperfect human beings. Christianity posits an omnipotent, omniscient, and omnipresent supreme being, an absolute ruler. In tribal societies, value systems are shaped by the expectations of the community. Tribal religions posit the existence of worlds whose present aspect is shaped by the action of a number of beings. The hills and valleys of the Cherokee homeland in central North Carolina were formed when a gigantic buzzard flew overhead and its wingtips hit the soft earth below.[23] The Navajo explain their presence in the central part of Arizona as the result of a migration through worlds below into this world, one that represents the cumulative creative actions of deities such as Black God, White Shell Woman, and Bogachiddy.[24]

The basic values in tribal communities come from a sense of human beings as part of the processes of the environment, an ongoing creation and re-creation of the world. These values reflect the involvement of human beings with the environment as hunters and subsistence farmers. Hopi sunwatchers on their mesas in central Arizona still carry out a ceremonial obligation to observe the horizon at sunrise and sunset to determine when the sun reaches its solstice points. The timing of key ceremonies in the Hopi yearly cycle depends upon this knowledge. The belief is that the sun is a spirit who moves from his summer house to his winter house over the course of the year. If human beings do not perform their ceremonies, the sun will not have the energy to rise from the house in which he rests at the solstice and resume his journey across the sky.[25]

The goal of life is maintaining a proper relationship with the spiritual world in order to achieve the ultimate goals of human life. If Christianity explores the notion of God, the study of ethics asks the question, What is good? The answer in Indian communities lies in two dimensions. For the individual, good is long life, good health, and happiness. It is achieved by remaining in proper relationship to all people, all beings in the physical world, and the spirits. The Navajo speak of *hozho*, a term generally glossed as "beauty," but which Gary Witherspoon defines as "the ideal environment of beauty, harmony, and happiness."[26] The ideal of harmony entails fulfilling one's responsibilities to the community and to the spirit world. The Chippewa term *pimidaziwin* translates as long life, good health, and happiness.[27] A Hopi man described the things that he would like to have happen in his life:

> To live a good life, to have rain, to live in plenty, no sickness, to live a long while until ready to go to sleep without pain, to have more livestock, to live with your wife without argument, to have money, to have fuel for the winter, to have dances so that we can amuse ourselves, to be a good weaver and make blankets and dresses, to have a nice patch of corn and beans, to dance, to live peaceably.[28]

The ultimate questions of reward and punishment that confound Christianity have relatively straightforward answers in Native communities. Illness in Hopi society, for instance, is thought of as a result of wrong behavior. Sin is "when you have children and they die. Of not being together, so that there's no rain. [friction in the village]."[29] For the Navajo, the ethical value system is totally self-referent. "There is no insis-

tence of impartiality, sympathy, benevolence, religious faith."
The concerns are for daily life and its outcomes.[30]

Christian theologians have equated human suffering with
human sinfulness. Native people have asked their own questions about the nature of the world. Aua, an Inuit man, asked
the Danish explorer Knud Rasmussen profound human questions about the meaning of human suffering in the world.
"Why are people hungry? . . . Why must people be ill and suffer
pain?" If people are not inherently evil, why must they suffer?
The equation of sin and suffering is deeply rooted in Western
society. Human beings must be punished in this world for sinful behavior. For Aua's people, however, the notion of suffering was based on fear of the unfamiliar and unknown, fear that
was kept at bay by following carefully prescribed behaviors
that represented the experience and wisdom of generations.
For Aua, "The greatest peril of life lies in the fact that human
food consists entirely of souls." All animals had souls that did
not die with their bodies but that must be carefully propitiated
lest they take revenge on humans.[31]

Sin from an Indian perspective can be defined as a failure to
live up to one's responsibility, sometimes deliberately but
more likely as a result of impulsive or unthinking behavior, a
mistake. In Christianity, sin has become privatized as a personal matter. For Indian people it is a matter of responsibility
to community. Those who do not participate in ceremonies
with appropriate thoughts may negate the effectiveness of the
ceremony to effect a restoration of appropriate relationships to
restore the whole community to well being.

Salvation can be defined as the ability of an individual or a
community to return to a state of communitas that has been
disrupted. The Cherokee had certain towns that were sacred
sites where people could seek sanctuary when they had transgressed social norms. The Green Corn Ceremony was a time of
forgiveness that restored all people (except murderers) to
proper relationships.[32]

The mechanisms for social control in Indian societies are
based in personal interactions rather than abstract rules.

Teasing and ridicule are common ways of letting people know that they are not doing the right thing. Sacred clowns represent the disorder in the universe that is antithetical to harmony and balance. Places remind the Cibecue Apache of appropriate behavior.[33]

Spirituality is a way of gaining access to power that can then be used for the good of the community. It defines the roles that people play in relation to other people. Ethical behavior is appropriate behavior.

The Sin of Pride

The Jesuits in colonial America wrote of their desire to "reduce" Indians through Christian education. The reluctance of Indians to submit to the Jesuits' instruction was viewed as the sin of pride, which in Catholic doctrine means considering one's self the equal of God.[34] What the Jesuits faced was an expression of the very basic principle of Indian beliefs concerning their relationship with the forces of the natural environment, that they were spirits with whom individuals could establish personal relationships through visions and dreams. When the notion of "personhood" includes plants, animals, stones, wind, water, stars, it is difficult to conceive of submission to a supreme being.

The Jesuits' reactions to Indian beliefs reveal the cultural gap that existed between Native belief systems and Christianity. What to the Christian mind was the sin of considering one's self as equal rather than subservient to God was, for Native people, appropriate behavior to maintain proper relationships with the spirits of the natural world. What Christian missionaries taught as the key to Christian salvation, Christ's birth and crucifixion, a group of Choctaws in Mississippi found "incomprehensible and almost beyond human belief." They could understand a friend dying for a friend, but they could not understand how a man could give his only son to die an excruciating death to benefit his enemies, a belief which ". . . filled them with wondering astonishment."[35]

The idea of sin as willful behavior that transgressed laws dictated by a supreme being contrasted sharply with the moral values of obligation and responsibility to one's family and community. Native people saw themselves not as subject to God but as active participants in the processes of the natural world. Their ceremonies and rituals were necessary to keep their worlds in balance and harmony, things that constituted the ultimate good. People must participate with good hearts and good thoughts, lest they offend the spirits and ruin the efficacy of the ceremony. To behave inappropriately was probably the closest equivalent to the Christian notion of sin in Native thought. It risked not only harm to the individual but to the community.

CHAPTER 7

TRICKSTER

The Sacred Fool[1]

Trickster was going along . . .

If one is to consider Native American Christian theology—
if one is to talk "god-talk" with a Native voice—then traditional theological categories must be reimagined and reformed
consistent with Native experience, values, and worldview. This
appropriation of the Gospel is no different from what believers
in any culture in any time have done. As Leonardo Boff re-
minds us, the Gospel is never "naked"; it is always culturally
clothed. Christians respond to the biblical witness because, to
paraphrase Coleridge, there is something that "finds them"
where they live their lives.[2] Unfortunately, too often Indians
were told that to become Christian meant to adopt Western
culture along with their baptism and to stop being Indian. Our
argument, however, goes beyond simply "revisioning" con-
ventional categories of Western systematic theology. It also
means considering new categories from Native thought-
worlds. One such new category is that of Trickster.

Actually, Trickster discourse is not a wholly new category.
In fact, it is not new at all but, rather, ancient. Many diverse

cultures around the world have trickster figures. "Trickster" is, in fact, an anthropological categorization, an abstraction from particular embodiments in different cultures. In West Africa, it is Anansi the spider. For the Greeks and Romans, he was Hermes or Mercury. In northern Europe, numerous stories are told about the trickster Loki. Native Hawaiians know him as Maui. It is among the Native nations of the Americas, however, that Trickster plays his most important role, taking on many guises—Raven, Iktomi the spider, Wolverine, Rabbit, and the most familiar trickster of all, Coyote. Who is this Trickster? What role does he play in indigenous cultures? And what does he have to do with a Native American theology?

The Reversal of the Ordinary

Lewis Hyde describes tricksters as

"on the road." They are the lords of in-between. A trickster does not live near the hearth; he does not live in the halls of justice, the soldier's tent, the shaman's hut, the monastery. He passes through each of these when there is a moment of silence, and he enlivens each with mischief, but he is not their guiding spirit. He is the spirit of the doorway leading out, and of the crossroad at the edge of town (the one where a little market springs up). He is the spirit of the road at dusk, the one that runs from one town to another and belongs to neither.[3]

Trickster, as his name implies, is a mischief maker. Though he is usually referred to as he, Trickster can easily switch gender. His sexual appetites are boundless, and he will seduce anything that moves, male or female. He makes trouble for everyone, including himself. Although Trickster may succeed in duping others, he as often comes to a bad end. Trickster stories teach what happens as a result of stupidity, gluttony, lust, and arrogance. Listeners laugh at his exploits, but they also learn societal values and mores through humor.

Indian readers will recognize the biblical story of Jacob (Gen 25:19–Gen 37) as a trickster cycle. Jacob contends with his twin, Esau, while still in the womb, grabbing his brother's heel to jockey for position and attempt to be the firstborn. Later, he tricks a ravenous Esau into selling his birthright for a mess of pottage. With the help of their mother, Rebekah, he poses as Esau to gain Isaac's blessing, rightly belonging to his brother. He deceives and cheats his father-in-law Laban out of his flock through a neat piece of trickery and then flees. Finally, he wrestles all night with Yahweh and comes away with a lame hip as a result of the combat.

The story of Jacob's duplicity in his dealings with Laban is reminiscent of a story told on the Atlantic Coast of Nicaragua, where the trickster of the Ashanti of Africa, Anansi, has melded with the culture of the Spanish and the local Miskito Indians and where today he is often called Hermano Anansi or Señor Anansi. As James De Sauza says of Anansi, "Sometimes he is a man; sometimes he is a spider. Sometimes he is good; sometimes he is bad. But he is always very, very tricky."[4] In the story, Anansi goes into the cattle business with Tiger—using Tiger's money. After a few years, they decide to split their large herd. After the division, Anansi tells his partner that it is too late to drive his herd away that night. He convinces Tiger to mark their respective cattle. Green leaves from the olive tree will be put on the ear's of Tiger's cows, while dead, brown leaves will be put on Anansi's. When the pair return, the fresh leaves have all turned brown, and Anansi departs with the entire herd, leaving Tiger broke and vowing revenge.

Trickster is a breaker of barriers, and an eraser of boundaries. He moves between heaven and earth, between deity and mortals, between the living and the dead. He is also the ultimate symbol of the ambiguity of good and evil and the essential statement of the human condition. Human beings may aspire to ultimate goodness, but they are subject to basic impulses and desires.

According to Hyde, "Sometimes it happens that the road between heaven and earth is not open, whereon trickster trav-

els not as a messenger [as Mercury/Hermes, the messenger of
the gods] but as a thief, the one who steals from the gods the
good things that humans need if they are to survive in this
world."

Raven, the trickster figure of the Northwest Coast, is a
good example of Hyde's point. Before Raven, the world is in
darkness. Through trickery, he steals light from the other
world and returns to earth with it. True to form, however, he
does this not out of any feeling for humanity but so that he will
have light to feed by.

The story illustrates Trickster's role as culture-hero, convey-
ing benefit on humankind. He is a creative figure, but he does
not create the world. Rather, he is a demiurge who shapes the
world and gives it form. Among the Haida, Raven is responsible for bringing the first humans into the world, changing his
raucous cawing to a soft coo and coaxing them from a clam-
shell. He is the one who teaches them to hunt and fish and
cook. He makes the first fishhook. He teaches the spider to
weave a web and then tells humans how to make nets in imita-
tion of the spider's lair.

Coyote teaches the Crow Indians how to hunt buffalo. He
teaches the Nez Perce how to net salmon. Sometimes, he takes
a more direct role in creation. Iktomi, the Spider trickster of
the Lakota, created time and space, language, and gave the animals their names. Glooskap, the Algonkian culture-hero,
shaped the rocky coast of New England. Maui pulls the Ha-
waiian Islands up from the bottom of the ocean. And among
the Innu of the Arctic, Wolverine is responsible for creation of
the land. He calls the sea beasts together and urges them to
bring earth from below the waters up to the surface of the primordial waters.

While not evil, Trickster can be cruel. In a Menominee
myth, for instance, Raccoon torments a pair of blind men.
Coyote is said by the Maidu of California to be the inventor of
the first lie and the Sioux consider Iktomi the "grandfather of
lies." Trickster can even be downright thuggish. Tseg'sgin', a
Cherokee trickster, has few, if any, redeeming qualities.

Some scholars have maintained that this Cherokee trickster is a relatively late development, post-dating contact with Whites. Jack and Anna Kilpatrick, in fact, surmise that "Tseg'sgin" (pronounced "Jegsgin") is a corruption of "Jackson," for Andrew Jackson, whose policy of removing Indians from the southeast led to the forced Cherokee march known as the Trail of Tears.[5]

The name of the Cheyenne Trickster "Veeho" means "white man,"[6] as does "Napi" in Blackfoot.[7] Like the Cherokee, the Blackfoot have another, more creative trickster, Coyote. These stories testify to the lability and continued vitality of trickster in Native life. Among the Maya of Guatemala, a newcomer is Maximon. Dressed in an ice cream white suit, Panama hat, and dark glasses, he is known as the Lord of Looking Good.

Negative aspects of Trickster are, however, not the norm. If Trickster is the "god" of chance, chance or luck are sometimes bad, as we all know, "and more often than not, overweening pride or overreaching control is a contributing factor" in the downfall of Trickster's victims, including himself.[8]

Trickster can brook no pretension. He punctures pomposity. He turns the world upside down, disordering the normal patterns of tribal life and values and subverting expectations. In this way, he helps keep the world imaginatively in balance. Richard Erdoes and Alfonso Ortiz describe the Hopi trickster, Masau'u:

> The Hopi god Masau'u, the Skeleton Man, is a creator, a germinator, the protector of travelers, the god of life and death, the peacemaker, and the granter of fertility. But he is also a lecher, a thief, a liar, and sometimes a cross-dresser. Masau'u is probably the strangest and most multifarious of all Native American trickster gods. He can assume any shape—human or animal—to lure a maiden to share his blanket. Ruler of the underworld, he is often shown as a skeleton but can also be depicted as a normal, handsome young man bedecked in turquoise. He is said to live in poverty, but he is lord of the land. . . . Masau'u is

also the boundary maker and the god of planting and agriculture. During Hopi planting ceremonies, a Masau'u impersonator is the center of the action.[9]

In fact, in the Southwest, sacred clowns are common. These performers, such as the *koshare* and *kwerana* among the Keresan Pueblos, exemplify the trickster. They disrupt and mock the solemnity of ceremonies, often in bawdy and Rabelaisian ways. According to Hyde, "Trickster the culture hero is always present; his seemingly asocial actions continue to keep our world lively and give it flexibility to endure. . . . I not only want to describe the imagination figured in the trickster myth. . . . the origins, liveliness, and durability of cultures require that there be space for figures whose function is to uncover and disrupt the very things that cultures are based on . . . *social life can depend on treating antisocial characters as a part of the sacred*."[10] Thus Trickster serves as an important social regulator.

There is, however, a built-in contradiction in Trickster. He is both sacred fool and sacred lecher. As the Sioux describe Iktomi, he may be mischievous and ribald, but he is nonetheless *wakan*, holy. Howard Norman says of trickster myths, "[T]hese tales enlighten an audience about the sacredness of life. In the naturalness of their form, they turn away from forced conclusions, they animate and enact, they shape, and reshape the world."[11] These stories and their enacted form in ritual teach the naturalness of humanity, including human sexuality. These lessons are reinforced by the fact that Trickster is usually envisioned as an animal. Natives traditionally do not see themselves as separated from the rest of the created order but as part of it.

This fact is illustrated by the very figures that different Native cultures chose to embody Trickster—spider, rabbit, coyote, raccoon, etc. All are animals that live in close proximity to humans but liminal to their settlements and thrive in that space. These are usually fast, getting in and out of human habitations quickly, appearing to come out of nowhere. They are often stealthy, sneaky, and thieving. Coyotes especially have shown themselves to be highly adaptive to human presence. They have learned to thwart Amer-European traps. And in the early American West, they were more social animals, hunting in packs like their cousins the wolf. Because wolves could not adapt to solitary hunts, they suffered, whereas the coyote adapted, able to hunt in either packs or alone, and flourished.

Lewis Hyde sums up:

> In short, trickster is a boundary-crosser. Every group has its edge, its sense of in and out, and trickster is always there, at the gates of the city and the gates of life, making sure there is commerce. He also attends the internal boundaries by which groups articulate their social life. We constantly distinguish—right and wrong, sacred and profane, clean and dirty, male and female, young and old, living and dead—and in every case trickster will cross the line and confuse the distinction. Trickster is the creative idiot, therefore, the wise fool, the gray-haired baby, the cross-dresser, the speaker of sacred profanities. When someone's honorable behavior has left him unable to act, trickster will appear to suggest an an amoral action, something right/wrong that will get life going again. Trickster is the mythic embodiment of ambiguity and ambivalence, doubleness and duplicity, contradiction and paradox.[12]

He concludes, "Here we have come back in a roundabout way to the earlier point: trickster belongs to polytheism or, lacking that, he needs at least a relationship to other powers, to people and institutions and traditions that can manage the odd double attitude of both insisting that their boundaries be respected and recognizing that in the long run their liveliness depends on having those boundaries regularly disturbed."[13] Can it be that modern society/the church/those in power/the West abhor such ambiguity and thus flee it?

The history of Christian/Native encounter would seem to indicate that this is, in fact, the case. Wakdjunkaga, the Winne-

Devil

bago trickster figure, may, in his early adventures, carry his
enormous penis around in a box (thus literally being "led
around by his dick"), but Christian missionaries were appalled
by such frank discussions of the earthiness of human existence.
This sexualized aspect of Trickster, coupled with his double-
ness, led these Christ-bearers to denounce the figure so central
to Native cultures. In their efforts to subvert and undermine
traditional Native concepts of deity, they equated and confused Trickster with Satan. Such was, however, calculated or
not, a misrepresentation. As Hyde points out, "The Devil is an
agent of evil, but trickster is *a*moral, not *im*moral. He embod-
ies and enacts that large portion of our experience where good
and evil are hopelessly intertwined. He represents the paradox-
ical category of sacred amorality."[14] Or according to Paul
Radin, the early anthropologist who recorded the Winnebago
trickster cycle, who generalizes: "Trickster is at one and the
same time creator and destroyer, giver and negator, he who
dupes others and is always duped himself. . . . He knows neither good nor evil yet he is responsible for both. He possesses
no values, moral or social . . . yet through his actions all values
come into being."[15]

Hyde concludes, "It might be argued that the passing of
such a seemingly confused figure marks an advance in the spiritual consciousness of the race, a finer tuning of moral judgment; but the opposite could be argued as well—that the era-
sure of trickster figures, or unthinking confusion of them with
the Devil, only serves to push the ambiguities of life into the
background. We may well hope that our actions carry no
moral ambiguity, but pretending that is the case when it isn't
does not lead to greater clarity about right and wrong; it more
likely leads to unconscious cruelty masked by inflated righ-
teousness."[16] Anyone familiar with the history of Christian/
Native encounter over more than five centuries will find little
to dispute in Hyde's assessment.[17]

The missionaries who branded the tricksters they encountered in Native cultures as demonic showed that they themselves were blind to the tricksters in the biblical tradition. Not

only is there an ancient Israelite trickster in the person of Jacob, but there are aspects of trickster evident in Jesus himself.

Jesus as Trickster

Jesus' trickster qualities were well recognized by early Christian authors as they searched for stories and metaphors to explain the Christ event. According to Luke's gospel, when Jesus was twelve, his parents take him to Jerusalem for Passover. After the festival, they depart for home, but Jesus has slipped away from them. Returning to the city to search for him, they find him three days later sitting among the teachers in the temple, listening and questioning them. When Mary asks him, "Child, why have you treated us like this? Look, your father and I have been searching for you in great anxiety," Jesus replies, "Why were you searching for me? Did you not know that I must be in my Father's house?" (Luke 2: 41-51). The incident is meant to illustrate Jesus' messianic mission from an early age. It is also, however, a trickster story. Jesus stealthily evades his parents and goes to the temple. When found out, his answer to his mother's question—which his parents did not understand—plays upon the term "father," his father being Joseph, and also Yahweh. In the non-canonical Gospel of the Infancy of Jesus, Jesus molds birds out of clay. When Joseph discovers him, he is furious that the boy is making idols. Jesus calls the birds to life and they fly away. For this author, it is a sign of the Messiah who does not yet understand his powers. Yet it is also the action of Trickster: caught in illicit activity, Jesus destroys the evidence of his transgression. Though the actions of Jesus with the birds would not conform to their image of Christ, immature or not, is it really that different, however, from the young Jesus, just beginning his ministry, who turns water into wine at the wedding at Cana? (John 2: 1-11).

Other aspects of Jesus career, demonstrate his affinity with Trickster. Trickster is perpetually on the move, just as Jesus is perpetually on the road, with no place to lay his head. Jesus is the antisocial disrupter of religious norms. He subverts expectations about not only what the Messiah is but what a holy person in first-century Palestine should be like. He loved a good party. He exercised his appetites and ate and drank with sinners and publicans. He deigned to have interaction with a despised Samaritan woman and preached of the good Samaritan, scandalizing the pious of his generation. He even gave healing, albeit reluctantly, to the Syro-Phoenician woman's child.

Healing is an important, but seldom understood, feature of trickster stories. Gerald Vizenor, the Native author who, more than any other, understands Trickster and writes about him with extreme sophistication, highlights this healing power. He offers readers compassionate tricksters who heal through story and humor.[18] Trickster stories are even sometimes used in healing rituals. Among the Navajo, according to Barre Toelken, "to tell such a story without such moral or medicinal motives does a kind of violence to it, and to the community."[19] Jesus' many healings may be mighty signs and wonders, but they also help mark him as Trickster.

In Matthew's gospel, the Pharisees seek to entrap Jesus. They go to him and ask if it is lawful to pay taxes to Caesar. It was a seemingly classic "no-win" situation. If Jesus said to pay taxes to Rome, he would infuriate Jewish nationalist interests. If he condemned the practice, he would be reported to Roman authorities for preaching sedition. But Jesus will not so easily be caught in the trap they have laid. He asks them to produce a coin and asks whose image is on it. When they reply, "Caesar's," he offers his retort, "Give to Caesar the things that are Caesar's, and give to God the things that are God's." The slippery Trickster has once again eluded his enemies. He will not so easily be captured and rendered tame.

Trickster is a boundary-crosser, who moves between heaven and earth, living and dead, opening up possibilities for humanity that would not exist but for his transgression of these limits. He is a god who "makes a way out of no way." In Jesus, Natives see the ultimate boundary-crosser, erasing the barriers between heaven and earth, life and death. In the resurrection, he becomes the *pontifex maximus*, literally the great bridge builder, building a bridge between life and life. Like Trickster, who is the spirit of the doorway leading out and the road beyond, Jesus is described as the "door" and the "way."

Finally, we see affinities with the tricksters and culture-heroes of Native America. Such figures often departed, and their return is anticipated. Passamaquoddy and Micmac stories document the withdrawal of Glooskap from his people. They make it clear, however, that he did not die but only retreated. In the Passamaquoddy story, he is in his lodge, making arrows; when the wigwam is filled with arrows, he will return to make war, signaling the eschaton. According to the Micmac, he will return to his people when Whites have departed. Though both stories are unmistakably post-Contact, there is little doubt that they reflect older traditions.

Tricksters do sometimes die. In one Cheyenne story, Veeho starves to death. Miguel Méndez, in his classic novel *Pilgrims in Aztlan*, gives us a Yaqui trickster, Rosario Cuamea, who dies trying to rape Death. Maui and Tseg'sgin' are reported to have perished in similar fashion. Yet, as Alan Velie points out, "[I]t is understood by teller and audience that trickster will be alive in the next episode."[20] To tell a story is to rehearse it, to re-enact it so that mythic time and chronological time merge. Sacred time is always present—in Native traditions as in Christianity.

Amer-European scholars are always ready to pronounce the oral traditions of Native cultures as artifacts. Hyde writes, "Outside of traditional contexts there are no modern tricksters because trickster only comes to life in the complex terrain of polytheism. If the spiritual world is dominated by a single high god opposed to a single embodiment of evil, then the ancient trickster disappears."[21] Yet, Native oral traditions, including those of Trickster, are very much alive. As with the Glooskap myths cited previous, they, like all living cultures, are constantly changing. Thus, in a Sioux myth, Coyote cheats a sharp-trading White man. In the Nicaraguan story cited above, Tiger gets his fortune, of which Hermano Anansi relieves him, by winning the lottery.

Trickster is in fact everywhere. He is Brer Rabbitt, a melding of West African traditions with the Cherokee's Jisdu. On a more mass culture level, he is even Bugs Bunny. Writers like Vizenor and Thomas King write stories and novels involving Trickster, thus continuing and changing the oral tradition. Trickster stories continue to be told to educate and entertain. Once more, Trickster has slipped through the fingers of those who would seek to destroy him.

We are not the first to suggest affinities between Jesus and Trickster. Sister Charles Palm, for example, in her book *Stories That Jesus Told: Dakota Way of Life*, draws parallels between specific myths involving Iktomi and Coyote and particular parables told by Jesus. She also rather curiously equates an incident in the career of the great Cheyenne culture-hero and prophet Sweet Medicine, who gave his people the Sacred Arrows with the parable of the sower and the seed.[22] Unlike her work, however, which drew simple and questionable equations in order to teach Sioux preschoolers Christian stories, we are making a more significant point. We affirm the sacrality of stories from the Native oral tradition. We do not suggest simple parallels between trickster stories and incidents reported by the gospel writers about the life and work of Jesus. We hope to show the importance of Trickster in Native cultures and open up a space for them to bring this part of their traditions into their Christian thinking and experience. By pointing out the trickster characteristics of Jacob or Jesus, we hope we illustrate that trickster discourse has something vital and important to tell us about the nature of the Christ event and of ultimate reality itself.

Trickster is a transgressor of boundaries and limits. He is a liar and a thief. Yet even this is to a purpose. Our ideas about property and theft depend on a set of assumptions about how the world is divided up. How did Joshua gain his advantages? Who gave Josiah's cattle to the White rancher in Leslie Marmon Silko's novel *Ceremony*? Trickster opens up the space to ask all the nasty, unanswerable questions about Amer-European occupation of the Americas. Trickster's lies and thefts challenge basic ethical premises of ownership, much as Indians question the ways in which Europeans gained possession of their lands.

The trickster makes artifice obvious but may also suggest alternatives. The West African trickster, Legba, mediates between truth and falsehood. A lie is really a truth, a deception that is in fact a revelation. Truth becomes lie, and vice versa. The point is that truth in the Christian sense cannot have absolute meaning in the minds of Indian Christians. Trickster and truth are far too slippery to be easily grasped.

Trickster transgresses boundaries and limits. He subverts expectations and disrupts social norms. Howard Norman writes, "His presence demands, cries out for, compassion and generosity toward existence itself. Trickster is a celebrator of life, a celebration of life, because by rallying against him a community discovers its own resilience and protective skills."[23]

Jesus, too, came enjoying and proclaiming life, and that abundantly. Like Trickster, he indulged his appetites. He feasted with his friends and enemies. He converted water into wine and drank of it. He was God, in his creative powers, and human in his appetites. Like the teachings of the Bible about human nature, Trickster stories are still an integral part of Indian traditions. They still teach societal mores and taboos and the dangers of ignoring them. But they are also, above all, entertaining. Mainstream Christians acknowledge Jesus' healings and compassion. They affirm his life and his Passion. Can they also embrace and revel in his humor and his passions? Can they believe in God as both constant and capricious? Can they recognize deity for the trickster that it is?

CHAPTER 8

Has a Spirit

LAND

We Sing the Land into Existence

*W*hen the Iroquois sang before their fires they believed they were helping to renew the world by giving strength to Teharonhiawagon, the Master of Life. The Iroquois believed the forest and everything in it was a living thing. Trees and wind and the smallest animals were important. Some creatures were so clever that they were considered to be related to the creative force which had made the universe. Songs in late winter, when life was harshest and men sometimes grew desperate in the bitter struggle to survive, were more than entertainment. Songs were a spiritual force that would help bring springtime when the forest would be reborn.[1]

Iroquois spirituality, like that of other Native Americans, was rooted in the land on which they lived. The natural environment was the embodiment of spiritual power. The forest was alive in both a literal and a figurative sense. This all-encompassing power was called by terms appropriate to each tribal entity, and the ceremonial relationship to a creator was appropriate to the respective nation. Where the European impulse to explore drove men across the Atlantic in the search for wealth, American Indian traditions tell of their origins in specific places, their emergence from worlds below or descent from the sky above to where they are now, or their migrations, led by spiritual guides, to homelands that were designated for them. This sense of a spiritual association with land, the marking of boundaries and renewal of the earth through ceremonies, and the concept of Earth as mother and nurturer, give land a special place in Indian senses of identity.

The spatiality that underlies Indian religious beliefs translates in contemporary American society into both cultural and political identity for Indian people. The term "earth" is most appropriate for a discussion of Native American spiritual concepts because it includes land, sea, and sky, and such presences as wind, rain, fire and light, as well as human and animal life. All of these elements of creation are of equal value in the Native American eye. For many Native American tribes, the earth is sacred and is itself a spiritual entity. It is not worshipped as a deity but, with the sky, seen as the source of physical and spiritual sustenance for the people. Everything the creator made is a living entity, and all things are related spiritually. Many Native people learned from childhood that the ground on which they walked was sacred ground. A Navajo dictionary of medical terms begins with the terms for feet because the feet touch the earth. This example stands in contrast to Western medicine's emphasis on the head as the source of rational knowledge.[2] The forest through which the Iroquois walked contained living beings made by the Creator and that these beings were the streams, and such living things as they could not see.

Traditionally, land was not thought of in terms of real estate to be bought, sold, or traded. The earth was a gift of the Creator given for the care of creation. The concept of the earth as the fructifying female manifestation of spiritual power, as "Grandmother" or "Mother," was drawn directly from Native peoples' understanding of their relationship to the creation in both its physical and spiritual manifestations.

Each people knew *their* land, their territory, in an intimate way. The boundaries of their land were always clearly defined; the people lived in harmony with the elements and the climate of their land; they knew intimately all of the foods and medicines available to them among the vegetation and the animals. Tribal people worked their lands in ways appropriate to their locale and terrain. The Iroquois planted their corn with a dead fish at the bottom of the planting hole. They piled earth around the base of the corn plants to protect them from predators. They planted different varieties of corn at different times to assure a continuous supply throughout the growing season. They attributed their plentiful harvests, however, to the Three Sisters, the spirits of corn, beans and squash who walked in their fields at night, their long hair and flowing garments touching the earth.[3] Human beings, animals, plants—all living things existed in a state of harmony.

Given the common bases for Native American spirituality, should we seek a Native American spiritual world view? The idea of a world view is an abstract and intellectual construct. We would have to do so respectfully recognizing a few limiting factors. Primary among these is the reluctance of many Native people to discuss in detail their tribal belief systems for publication. The fear is that transmitting such information is a function of the elders and also that such information might be corrupted in translation from oral tradition to written form. What remains then is information that has been shared and which has become common knowledge or understanding. A case for at least an introduction to a world view can be made because of the fact that Native American spirituality is important and should be respected as any other faith is respected.

The term Earth encompasses the land and sea and atmosphere, the wind, the rain, the thunder, the lightning, the receptor of the life-giving power of the Sun and the benefits of the moon. It is the vantage point from which we view the Sun, Moon and Stars and other wonders of the sky. The Earth is regenerative and can recover from any harm done by the inhabitants.

"Land" is the name given in the respective languages to designate that specific portion of Spirit Earth on which a particular nation resides. Native American world views become distinctive when oral traditions explain how a particular people came to be in the particular place in which they live. For some, like the Navajo and Hopi in the southwest, stories tell of their emergence from the earth itself into this world.[4] The Pawnee tell how they came from the stars, and their villages were oriented to the patterns of the stars and the rising sun.[5] The Seneca origin tradition begins in a world above this and tells how a woman fell through a hole in the earth above and was placed on the back of a turtle who rose from the ocean below. The turtle's back became the new earth for the Seneca.[6]

In the Native American traditional sense the earth must be thought of in a qualitative sense rather than in a quantitative sense. It was by living in harmony with the earth that Native peoples were able to find sustenance wherever they lived on the continent. There were no waste lands, no impotent lands. The "people" could always find ways to enjoin the powers of the Earth to provide the essentials for their livelihood.

In the Southwest region of North America, Amer-Europeans found the land hostile and overwhelmingly arid. The resident Native peoples, however, had great respect for the land of their ancestors. The Grand Canyon region was designated "Great Painted Lady." "It is a vast and quiet region, but to the Indians who made it their home, there was no such thing as emptiness. Everything was alive with spirit power. Even the heavens above were filled with the wandering souls of the dead and numberless supernatural beings. Only in some remote spot or in some sheltered silence of the night could the voices of these spirits be heard. Only by tireless contemplation could the totality and unity of all life be understood."[7] Every inch of the earth's surface contained elements of survival for people who respected the land. That is why the Pueblo and other Southwestern tribes could develop well-cared-for communities in areas of the Southwest that Europeans found dreadful and unforgiving.

The Howling Wilderness

It is clear that the Native and European cultures that encountered each other in North and South America related differently to the land. On the Great Plains of the central United States, as John Opie argues, Indians had made their presence felt for centuries: "Since about A.D. 1000, the argument goes, the existence of the American grasslands may well be ascribable to a man-nature symbiosis. The American Indian, for example, can be described as a major agent in a biotic system that he maintained to his satisfaction by repeated human intervention." White homesteaders, Opie continues, "Initially . . . avoided the mid-continent grasslands. They believed that the region was a desert, unable to support anything but the prairie grass, since it could not support trees. They called the prairie *the Great Obstacle*."[8]

In the forests of Europeans, from which the immigrants came, the most common task was to clear trees so that whatever caused trees to grow would cause crops to grow. "Hence the White settler who arrived on the Western plains was truly a stranger in a strange land (North America)." Later immigrants, probably out of necessity, discovered the value of the grasslands, and better farm equipment allowed them to farm them.

Earlier immigrants traveling westward through the heavily forested areas of the eastern mountains became conscious of the sounds of living things by day, sounds which seemingly were magnified at night. The calls of numerous varieties of animals created a din of noise, so much so that European immigrants called these forests "the howling wilderness." The forests were indeed wild and would have to be cleared so humans could inhabit the land. Historians have tended to reinforce the idea that North America was a vast, empty land—there for the taking.

As Opie points out "The presence of the Indian, of course, precluded any valid notion of a land devoid of human occupancy. But, until recently, frontier historians wrote as if the

Native inhabitants did not significantly modify the landscape. The argument was that, if the Indian was unable to stand up against white intervention, surely he was culturally weak and technologically helpless before the environment as well. Indian cultures were sophisticated, however, and had their own priorities over intensive land use. Frontier history is more adequately described in part as a contest between remarkably different cultures for the use of a landscape."[9]

"Wilderness" is most probably a term which is without meaning in a traditional Native community since, regardless of the habitat, whether desert or forest or plains encountered by the white immigrants, it had already been accounted for by the Native peoples who drew from that habitat the resources needed by the community. The absence of "ruins" of living organisms and cultures caused the immigrants to speak of a vast, empty land. Travelers reported traveling for days through a territory without encountering Native peoples, although they may well have been observed and followed by the Native people through whose territory they were passing. Indians on the Plains traveled lightly upon the land and left few signs of their passage.

A Problematic Historical Context

Histories of American lands have been written by Amer-European historians to explain how land has been modified and commodified.[10] For Native Americans who derived their subsistence and spirituality from the land, the very term "history" has no meaning. The Amer-European view of history is that it records progress and change, whereas Indians valued the repetition of events—the growth of crops, the mating seasons for animals, the recurrent patterns of rainfall.

Whose "history" forms an appropriate context for a discussion of land? Is there a Native American history apart from Amer-European history. One might think that history is history regardless of the various actors who enter the passing scene narrative. But in fact there is a lively discussion found in the writings of several non-Indian writers who have made significant contributions to our understanding of the role of Native Americans in American history.

Reginald Horsman argues for a distinctive Native American history that derives out of the cultural experience of Native societies. That history should not be written only from the written documents that are the accepted source of historical research, but from an understanding of Native views. He proposes that portraying Native peoples as victims of European aggression is not a productive way of writing history. Instead, he suggests that a global comparison of the impact of European colonization on Native cultures will reveal the fundamental differences in world view that underlay the results of European conquest.[11]

For Native Americans, it must be remembered that the American colonial government justified its existence by vilifying English government policies, specifically maintaining peaceful relations with Indian tribes who were perceived as a threat to American colonists. The colonists' complaints about Indian depredations were among those that led to the Revolutionary War.

Native American history has in the past been largely expunged from textbooks and studies in public schools, colleges, and universities. White historians have much to explain about how they can write hundreds of volumes about White expansion on Native American land without so much as mentioning the presence of Native American societies existing between the east coast and the west coast. How can they write about exploration and prospecting for precious metals and profitable mineral deposits without mentioning the encroachment on and theft of Native American homelands where that wealth was found?

It may be that Reginald Horsman, Robert Berkhofer, and others have introduced a new approach to Native American history because the discussion has focused on the philosophy of history. A major issue that should be of concern to historians and theologians is how Amer-Europeans have used history to justify their presence and their control of lands on the North and South American continents in the face of extensive Indian occupation of those lands. From the *Requiermiento* of 1513, the document that Spanish admirals read to the empty coast-lines of lands that they claimed for their sovereigns, to John Marshall's decision in the M'Intosh case in 1823, that Europeans had the right of discovery to take title to land, while Indians had only a right of occupancy, history has been bent to the advantage of the conqueror.[12] Europeans reduced the relationship of Indian people to their lands from a spiritual reality to a legal fiction. A reasonable approach to the troublesome issue might go a long way toward promoting a hopeful future for all sides as we turn to face the Creator.

Culture and Conversion

Culture becomes a defining element in reconciling the attitudes of Europeans and Native people toward the land. Native peoples, confronted with Christian beliefs, had to find a way of dealing with new ideas. The most common perception among religious spokespersons is that one moves from one system of belief (religion) to another by a process called conversion. Conversion implies the conscious act of dropping one's allegiance to one's original set of beliefs and declaring allegiance to another belief system. Whether such perfect conversions take place is problematic. It is not reasonable to expect that any human being is ever able, consciously or not, to jettison all the cultural and spiritual baggage of past experience.

Given the differences in world view, and also the fact that Native people live today in American society, and that their lives have been changed by their contact with Amer-Europeans, how can traditional beliefs be reconciled with Christianity? Like all peoples, Native people must connect with the work of the Creator, which has continued despite their historical ordeal. If Native people choose to become

Christian, they still have a responsibility to the Creator, whom they can also accept as the Christian God. They must become interpreters of the faith and good stewards of Native traditional spirituality as it is manifest in the land. They must realize that their relationship with the land is an on-going process that sustains their spirituality. Their ceremonial activities are an integral part of the natural environment, indeed are causal. Rather than rote request, ceremonies renew the land and human relationship with it.

The Mescalero Apache tribe in the southwest mark young women's first menses with a ceremony that celebrates their womanhood and ability to give birth. The ceremony also shapes them physically into models of Apache women through massage, the act of running, and the act of grinding corn. An integral part of the ceremony is the series of songs that are sung in the tipi on the last night of the ceremony. The final song ends just as the sun rises, and it is understood that the singer has the power to pull the sun over the horizon.[13]

Legal Constructs of Indian Land

The Amer-European view of Indian land was embedded in legal concepts that had no meaning in traditional Indian cultures. Those concepts are apparent in legal decisions that determined the fate of Indian lands. In the United States Supreme Court decision in the case of *Caldwell vs. the State of Alabama* (1832), the issue was whether the white government of the State of Alabama had jurisdiction in Creek Territory. The Creek Tribe claimed jurisdiction based on prior occupancy and governmental sovereignty. The tribe asserted that "possession acquired by force conferred no right" to Alabama since the state violated the "paramount natural right of the original occupants."[14] Chief Justice Lipscomb dismissed the Creek claims with contempt. "We will examine this high pretension to savage sovereignty. If a people are found in the possession of a territory, in the practice of the arts of civilization, employed in the cultivation of the soil, and with an organized government, no matter what may be its form, they form an independent community; their rights shall be respected and their territorial limits not encroached on." Notwithstanding that the Creek Nation could thus be described in 1832, the justice declared that they were one of a number of "savage tribes without a written language, or established form of government, and wholly ignorant of the customs and usages of civil society, (and) are not capable of appreciating the principles of their code."[15] Extending his remarks to include all Native American nations, in spite of the fact that he was ignorant of the governmental structure of the Creek Nation, he declared all tribes to be wandering hunters (not even descriptive of the Creek tribe) and one might just as well make a treaty with "the beast of the same forest that he inhabits."[16]

Justice Taylor reinforced, in a more scholarly way, the views of Justice Lipscomb. He asserted the right of European immigrants to take land from the original inhabitants of the American continent by appealing to the "right of discovery," the doctrine that John Marshall enunciated in the M'Intosh decision. He also asserted the right of military conquest as a means of acquiring land from Native people when needed on other occasions, and the right to acquire land by purchase from Native tribes. He asserted that "most" land was acquired by purchase while admitting that where purchase actually took place, the amount given was insufficient to confirm a serious claim by the purchaser. Furthermore, the Native parties to the purchase were unfamiliar with the concept of land as a subject of barter.[17]

As Tecumseh once declared "Sell land? You might as well sell air and water!" Modern descendants of the American colonies have achieved that feat. Air pollution and the destruction of surface fresh water and the pollution of underground aquifers have resulted in costly efforts to allow human beings to breathe air and drink water safely.

The decisions of the Supreme Court in the nineteenth century demonstrate the gulf that existed between Native people and American concepts of land and Native cultures. The Court simply dismissed the notion of a Native sovereign government and appealed only to European legal concepts, and where precedent was missing they created concepts which they claimed were rooted in European law. The favorite claim of the colonial mind both then and now is that Native people are politically, philosophically, and even spiritually without strength.

Commenting on contracts and agreements in the northeastern colonies between Whites and Native people, Justice Taylor wrote: "These people, chiefs and all, are like infants, pronounced incapable of protecting their own interests. Yet these persons, who have not a sufficient capacity to be permitted to make a binding contract to the amount of a dollar, are intelligent enough to estimate their national interests; to meet the learned and wily European as diplomat, make treaties by which they are again and again yielding up millions of acres of fertile land and all this is done on terms perfectly reciprocal . . . and the ignorance of the red man causes him to sell!" Often that was not the case. Instead, it was the ignorance of the white man which caused him to believe that he was buying land from a people whose culture and practices did not allow for the selling of land.[18]

As far as the argument of land secured by conquest, Taylor himself points out that the United States government had never declared war on Native tribes so there is no conqueror or conquered status involved. In the latter part of the nineteenth century certain military leaders took it upon themselves to attempt the extermination of Native peoples, but not because of an open declaration of war by the U.S. Government. It was egotistic bigotry that led to the inhumane actions of Custer and General Sheridan.

"Let Him Begin without Lands"

"I suppose the end to be gained however far away it may be, is the complete civilization of the Indian and his absorption into our national life . . . The Indian to lose his identity as such, to give up his tribal relations and to be made to feel that he is an American citizen . . . The sooner all tribal relations are broken up; the sooner the Indian loses all his Indian ways, even his language, the better it will be for him and for the (U.S.) government. To accomplish that, his removal and personal isolation is necessary. It would be kindness to give him education and industrial training and let him begin without lands."[19]

At the turn of the twentieth century, military officer Richard Pratt was influential in the formulation of U.S. Government policy for Native American tribes. He supported the initiative of Senator Henry Dawes to pass legislation to break up Indian reservations as communal land holdings and allot them as individual 160 acre plots to Indian heads of families, their dependent children, and single individuals over 18 years of age. Title to the land would be held in trust by the government for 25 years while Indians learned to farm and to manage their own affairs.

Dawes's bill was designed to assimilate Indians into American society as farmers, but it ultimately led to the loss of the majority of Indian lands.[20] Pratt's notion of stripping Native American people of their land indicates that he realized the importance of land in Indian cultures. In 1879 he had established Carlisle Indian School in order to remove Indian children from their native cultures so they could be educated in the ways of American society. He declared his intent to "kill the Indian to save the man."[21]

In the late nineteenth century, the perception was that Indians must be assimilated, or they faced extermination. The nadir of Indian population, about 250,000 in 1890, indicates the seriousness of the situation. Pratt's intention to strip Indians of all resources and educate them in American ways was an important principle in his thinking. Not all members of Congress agreed with him. Senator Morgan opposed an early version of Dawes's bill, pointing out that the ability of the Southwestern tribes was more than adequate to provide more than mere subsistence for the people of the various tribal communities: "So much respect has been paid to the communal idea, the tribal government of these Indians in our treaty relations with them and in our statutory enactments heretofore, that we have not seen proper to disturb anything of that kind; and I venture to say that plenty of instance can be found of treaties solemnly entered into between us and the Indian tribes which will be plainly violated if this law (allotment act) is passed."[22]

Senator Teller of Colorado predicted the outcome of the legislation. "You propose to divide all their land and to give each Indian his quarter section . . . And for twenty-five years he is not to sell it or dispose of it in any shape, and at the end of that time he may sell it. It is safe to predict that when that shall have been done, in thirty years thereafter there will not be an Indian on the continent, or there will be very few at least, that will have any land."[23]

The General Allotment Act led to the loss of one hundred million acres of Indian land between 1887 and 1934, when the allotment policy was reversed by the Indian Reorganization Act. As Deloria commented, "Teller ended his speech with a prophecy that Indians will curse the day when people wanted them to allot their lands. The day has long since come. Today younger Indians are coming to realize that the kindly old missionaries were really land agents who helped rape the tribe of its land base."[24]

Essential to the survival of the Southwestern tribes was the "communal idea" spoken of by Senator Morgan. It was the communal system that enabled the tribal groups to produce crops and fill storehouses to sustain the people on a continual basis. And it was also the communal system that stood in the way of the European exploiters. The senator's description of the successful agrarian practices of the Pueblo fell on deaf ears: "Now, take the twenty-seven pueblo tribes down in the Arizona desert. You may pass over that desert and find cornfields, and when you are approaching you see the tassels of the corn, when in full tassel not more than a foot above the ground. You will find the Indian has scooped out a basin of two or three feet, in which he has planted the seed for the purpose of getting moisture by capillary attraction, there being no rains in that country and no chance for irrigation; and there they raise a hard corn of excellent character, corn that will keep better than any we have in our country, and not corn merely, but wheat, and an abundance of it; and there is not one of those pueblos that has not a year's supply for every man, woman and child laid up in advance."[25]

The Dawes Act was and is considered one of the most destructive pieces of legislation enacted by the United States Congress. It has become a touchstone for contemporary American Indian activists. Winona LaDuke (White Earth Ojibwe) asserts that "the process of allotment was one of the single more destructive pieces of legislation passed by the U.S. Government, causing Indian communities to lose two-thirds of all reservation land nationally . . . and opened remaining lands for homesteading (by whites)."[26] The Allotment Act was particularly destructive because Native people were caught in the breech between their traditional spiritual associations with land and American values of land as a commodity to be exploited for financial reasons.

Most Native peoples were not aware that particular geographic areas in which they lived were being claimed by a foreign people as exclusive territories. Many adults who were aware of what was happening refused to participate in the allotment system and thus lost any claims to land. In Oklahoma a version of the Indian land allotment system known as the Indian Welfare Act was put into effect. The tribal rolls were closed and tribal territories were broken up into land parcels and assigned to tribal members without legal protection. Indian babies on the rolls received allotments and were assigned white guardians. By the time these infant assignees reached legal age, their land had often passed to the ownership of the "guardian."

The intent of the Dawes Act is best characterized by President Theodore Roosevelt, who declared in his annual message to Congress in 1901 that the act was "a mighty pulverizing engine to break up the tribal mass."[27] The mass remains, however, because the opening of reservations proceeded on the basis of reservation by reservation legislation, and not all the lands declared as surplus by the act were actually claimed by Amer-European settlers. In 1934, the Indian Reorganization Act took those lands back into trust status for tribes. Despite the fact that contemporary reservation boundaries may encompass numerous tracts owned by non-Indians, the concept of reservation land as homeland is strong in Indian country.

Contemporary Issues with Regard to Land

Despite the loss of Indian land, Native American survival as a people in contemporary America has unquestionably been due to tribal traditions. The spiritual traditions of a people are not as easily subject to material politics as the land base is. And much of the remaining land base was protected because of the temporal survival of the tribe.

The Lakota land claims to the Black Hills in South Dakota emphasize these distinctions. The Black Hills were sacred to the Lakota as a source of spiritual power. Certain sites were used for vision questing by young men seeking spiritual power. The Hills were the home of those spirits. Ceremonial pilgrimages every year also allowed tribal elders to follow the path of the stars through the sky (the Zodiac) and relate it to the physical terrain of the hills.[28]

In 1868, after successfully fighting the encroachment of the United States army and white gold prospectors, the Lakota bands led by Red Cloud signed a treaty ceding some of their lands but reserving forever the western two thirds of what is now the state of South Dakota, including the Black Hills.[29] The subsequent discovery of gold in the Black Hills led to an influx of white prospectors, and Lakota resistance led the United States government to send troops to subdue them. George Armstrong Custer led a contingent of troops to the fatal encounter at the Little Big Horn river in 1876. The fate of Custer's men received widespread media coverage. American was celebrating the 100th anniversary of its founding. The defeat of American military forces by Indians raised national outrage. The retaliation was swift, and by 1877, military defeats forced the Lakota to sign treaties agreeing to cede even the Black Hills.[30]

The Lakota brought a suit before the U.S. Court of Claims seeking return of their lands. They based their argument on a provision of the 1868 treaty that no subsequent changes could be made without the agreement of three-fourths of the adult males of the tribe. The Court agreed that the 1868 treaty had been violated and issued a monetary judgment. But what the Lakota want is the land that they consider as a source of their spiritual power.[31]

The Black Hills represent the complexity of contemporary Native identity with land. In a spiritual sense, the Hills are a source of power. In a historical sense, they have been used by Lakota people. In a legal sense, their ownership has been determined by treaties between the Lakota and the United States government. In a political sense, the governments of the Lakota reservations in South Dakota have refused to accept the monetary judgment of the Court of Claims.[32]

Christians do not think of themselves as belonging to the land, especially when it has been reduced to a commodity. They sing, "This land is not my home—I's just a-passing through. If Heaven's not my home, O Lord what will I do?" Christians seem to believe that the firmament created by the sovereign God is less than sufficient for humanity. Earth is simply a stopping place on the way to heaven, rather than being a source of identity as it is for Indian people.

Redefining Land

The need for careful and thoughtful hermeneutics is demonstrated in a popular new translation of the New Testament and the Psalms. Compare Psalm 90 in the New International Version and New English Bible translations with the same passage in Eugene H. Peterson's translation of the same passage. From the New International Version:

> Lord, you have been our dwelling place
> throughout all generations.
> Before the mountains were born
> Or you brought forth the earth and the world,
> From everlasting to everlasting you are God.
> You turn men back to dust,
> Saying, "Return to dust, O sons of men."
> For a thousand years in your sight
> are like a day that has just gone by,
> or like a watch in the night.
> You sweep men away in the sleep of death;
> They are like the new grass of the morning—
> though in the morning it springs up new
> by evening it is dry and withered.

From the New English Bible:

> Lord, thou hast been our refuge
> from generation to generation,
> Before the mountains were brought forth,
> or earth and world were born in travail,
> from age to age everlasting thou art God.
> Thou turnest man back into dust;
> 'Turn back,' thou sayest, 'you sons of men';
> for in thy sight a thousand years are as yesterday;
> a night-watch passes, and thou hast cut them off;
> they are like a dream at daybreak,
> they fade like grass which springs up with the
>   morning
> but when evening comes is parched and withered.

From Peterson's translation of the same passage:

God, it seems you've been our home forever;
Long before the mountains were born,
Long before you brought earth itself to birth,
From "Once upon a time" to "Kingdom come"
You are God.
So don't return us to mud, saying,
"Back to where you came from!"
Patience! You've got all the time in the world—
Whether a thousand years or a day.
Its all the same to you.
Are we no more to you than a wispy dream?
No more than a blade of grass
That springs up gloriously with the rising sun
And is cut down without a second thought?

Peterson has transformed a penitent psalmist into a bitter prosecutor of the Creator. Never mind that he also mangled some grand poetry of the Old Testament. In dismissing the fertility of the land as a fleeting thing, he dismisses the possibility of spirituality based on a relationship with natural processes. If natural phenomena are ephemeral, the Native cultural systems based upon relationships with those phenomena become also ephemeral. This attitude toward the land in Christian thought reflects the philosophy of Amer-Europeans that have influenced United States policy, the allotment policy, and the attempt to destroy traditional Native ways of association with the earth. Because of government policies, tribes were not able to find ways to utilize their resources to adapt to a new political and economic status in American society. Only in recent years have a few tribes launched their own efforts to develop themselves economically and politically.

The Native American reverence for earth and the spirituality of all living things persists even today and is often expressed. The Western Shoshone people have struggled to prevent their homelands from becoming a dumping ground for toxic wastes. Other Native peoples have sought to protect sacred places as well as to protect the earth from intentional harm. Richard Pratt, the military officer who developed the U.S. boarding school system for the purpose of dispossessing Native Americans of their culture, land, and souls partially succeeded because of the Allotment Act and because his boarding school system became a model for the education of Native American students. On the other hand, some public education experiences have led intelligent young Native Americans to seek greater understanding of their culture and their current relation to it and the dominant society in which they must live.

Contemporary Native American activists are seeking to protect the remaining land base, and in some cases they are attempting to extend the land base by purchase and reclamation. Winona LaDuke, Director of the Land Recovery Project on the White Earth Chippewa Reservation in Minnesota, is an outspoken advocate for extending the land base of Indigenous peoples: "That is what Indian people are doing throughout the country. We are working in all arenas that we need to recover the land that we had. What do we do in a larger context? It is incumbent upon each of us to begin the process of redrawing geography in whatever arena that is. I believe that is how you view the world. If we view Central and South America as small White countries, we never actually discuss the fact that in many of those countries the majority population is Native. An indigenous geography should be a critical part of world geography and the view that we all collectively have of the world."[33]

LaDuke explains traditional Ojibwe geography as follows: "Inside our reservations we maintain a traditional system of land management and indigenous natural resource management practices that are different from European common law. Our practice is collective ownership and individual or extended family use rights. Does this mean anything to you? Collective ownership, individual family or extended usufruct rights. The idea is that you don't own it, but you have a right to harvest there so in our traditional area, for instance, many of the use rights were non-contiguous parcels. Maybe I'd get my wild rice over here and my maple sugar bushes over here. I go over here and that is where my trapline is."[34]

Many contemporary tribes use a similar communal system. Land in the traditional sense is managed for the benefit of the tribe and land management includes economic and community development and family home sites. The concept of "ownership" of land is a concession by the contemporary Native tribal system, another political predicament. The traditional perception of Native American indigenous people is that you cannot "sell" land in the European sense because you cannot "own" it as Europeans claim. The "use" of land is what is available to tribal members. In contemporary times, however, one speaks of "ownership" to protect a given territory for use by the present occupants. As far as the surface of the earth is concerned, it cannot be drawn and quartered and sold to the highest bidder.

The importance of land as a source of identity is evident in the following story. A young man traveling in his familiar homeland, the Southwest, came upon a young man, a traveler from Central America who was near death from exposure and lack of food and water. The first young man took the traveler back to his village, performed healing ceremonies for him, treated him according to ways he was taught by the elders. Soon the traveler responded. He was given food and water. After several days the Central American traveler regained his strength and was ready to continue his journey. He was given supplies and prayers for a safe journey. Their languages were different and at no time did they understand each other by language, but there apparently was no barrier in their spiritual communication.

Native people generally recognize a kinship among all Native peoples which is fundamentally spiritual in nature. In today's world where strangers dominate, a Native American person traveling in a large city far from home may find himself staring intently at a face in the crowd wondering if the person is a Native person. Native people serving in the U.S. armed forces often seek each other out, sometimes approaching a total stranger and asking if he is a Native American (some say "Indian"). The next question is predictable. "What tribe?" This universal sense of kinship among Native Americans may reflect the communal nature of the spiritual traditions of the respective tribes.

Christian Attitudes Toward Native Spirituality

Although contemporary Christian churches have established missions to Indian congregations and in some cases have made attempts to foster the integration of Indian and Christian practices, there are still vestiges of older Christian feelings toward traditional religions. Winona LaDuke tells us how contemporary people are reasserting their claims to the land. "You see that particularly in our region, with the recovery of indigenous people that were called the *Devil's Lake Sioux*. When Christians came they saw Indian religions and native religious practice and they did not like it. So what was Native, what was 'Spirit Lake,' was named Devil's Lake (by Whites). So the Devil's Lake Sioux have renamed their lake Spirit Lake and their band as Spirit Lake Lakota. That is indicative of part of that reclaiming process that is going on in our Native communities."[35]

Throughout the United States, Native place names for sacred and ceremonial places were become designated as Devil's Lake, Devil's highway, Devil's Canyon. Christians who gave places these names assumed that those associations with Indian beliefs gave them demonic qualities. They could not understand the profound emotional association that Native people felt with their lands. They would not have understood the Umatilla Headman who said: "I have only one heart. Although you say go to another country, my heart is not that way. I am here, and here is where I am going to be. I will not part with my lands. If you come again, I will say the same things. I will not part with my lands."

Native Americans and Environmental Concerns

Traditional Indian values with regard to land have been adapted by contemporary environmental movements. The respect for the land that is characteristic of Indian societies has its appeal for Americans who see that human action has led to pollution of land and water in ways that threaten the future quality of life for all human beings. A speech attributed to Seattle, Headman of the Suqwamish and Duwamish at treaty negoations at Port Elliot, Washington in 1855, was widely appropriated by environmental groups during the 1970s. Although it proved to be the creation of a screenwriter in 1972 rather than Seattle's actual words from 1855, it captured a spirit that is true to traditional Native beliefs with regard to the earth.

"Our religion is the tradition of our ancestors—the dreams of our old men, given to them in the solemn hours of night by the Great Spirit; and the visions of our sachems are written in the hearts of our people. Your dead cease to love you and the land of their nativity as soon as they pass the portals of the tomb and wander way beyond the stars. Our dead never forget the beautiful world that gave them being. Every part of this soil is sacred in the estimation of my people. Every hillside, every valley, every plain and grove has been hallowed by some sad or happy event in days long vanished. Even the rocks which seem to be dumb and dead as they swelter in the sun along the silent shore, thrill with memories of stirring events connected with the lives of my people, and the very dust upon which you now stand responds more lovingly to their footsteps than to yours, because it is rich with the blood of our ancestors and our bare feet are conscious of the sympathetic touch. . . . and when the last Red Man shall have perished, and the memory of my tribe shall have become a myth among the white man, these shores will remain with the invisible dead of my tribe, and when your children's children think themselves alone in the field, the store, the shop, upon the highway, or in the silence of the pathless woods, they will not be alone. In all the earth there is no place dedicated to solitude. At night when the streets of your cities and villages are silent and you think them deserted, they will throng with the returning hosts that once filled and still love this beautiful land."[36]

Although the preemption of the speech by non-Indians distorts history, it does offer the hope that future generations of Native Americans and Amer-Europeans might work together to restore a balance between humans and the Earth that nurtures them.

The land upon which Native people lived, and which they respected, has been the site of contest between those people and the European colonizers who came to appropriate it. Native people have adapted their belief systems because of education and Christian beliefs that have allowed them to find new ways of expressing their feelings toward the Earth and the Creator. The reconciliation of traditional beliefs and Christian theology has helped Native communities retain a sense of their cultural identities. God, Creator, and Earth, can be seen as part of the greater whole of human existence.

CHAPTER 9

ESCHATOLOGY
End, Salvation, Rebirth[1]

*W*hen Jesus came into the coasts of Caesarea
Philippi, he asked his disciples, saying, Whom do
men say that I the Son of man am? And they said, Some say
that thou art John the Baptist; some, Elijah; and others,
Jeremias, or one of the prophets. He saith unto them, But
whom say ye that I am? And Simon Peter answered and
said, Thou art the Christ, the Son of the living God.

                                        Matthew 16:13-16 KJV

The theologian Paul Tillich places the essence of Christianity in this dialogue between Jesus and his apostle Peter on the road to Caesarea Philippi. Peter asks, Who are you? Jesus's query to Peter is "Who do *you* say I am? Peter answers Jesus' query: "Thou art the Christ."[2] We would contend that the importance of the event lies not in Peter's answer but in the question itself. This is the question put before every Christian at every time. The question Native Christians must ask is "Who do *we* say he is?"

Native people must travel a road toward Christianity different from traditional ones.[3] The task for Native Christians is to discern the Christ of the Red Road. We have suggested some ways that they respond to this task in the chapter on Christology. We now conclude in this chapter dealing with eschatology.

The final chapter of traditional studies of systematics deals with eschatology. It is that branch of theology that concerns death, the state of the soul after death, final judgment, and last things. As such it also concerns ultimate salvation. This volume is somewhat divergent in that here it is the penultimate entry. We are sufficiently concerned to root this systematic theology in this time and place and in the diverse cultures of Native America that we conclude with a chapter on contemporary issues.

When speaking of a Native theology, capable of embracing, as much as possible, the entire Native community, a problem immediately arises with regard to ultimate salvation. Native American religious traditions are not "religions" of dogma or theology. Rather, they are, like Shinto, religions of ritual observance. Unlike Islam or Christianity, they are not salvific faiths. They are totally centered on and in the community. As we have noted, the closest approximation of the Christian notion of sin in Native traditions is a failure to live up to one's responsibilities to the community. Likewise, that most approximating "salvation" is the continuance of the community.[4]

While one cannot intelligibly discuss salvation with regard to Native traditions, it is possible to talk about eschatology with regard to Native traditions. Despite the early disparaging comments of ethnographers and scholars of comparative religion, most tribal nations had developed notions of death and the afterlife. Some believe in the transmigration of souls. While many orthodox Christians are swift to point out that belief in reincarnation is not a Christian concept, such a statement is either disingenuous or historically naïve. When Jesus questions his disciples at Caesarea Philippi, first asking who do people say the Son of Man is, they reply, "Some say John the Baptist, some Elijah, and others Jeremiah or one of the prophets." As theologian Leslie Weatherhead puts it, "Is it not extraordinary that he did not tell them not to talk nonsense" if reincarnation were impossible?[5] In fact, first-century Jews, awaiting the Messiah, expected that Elijah must return first. Origen, Augustine, Jerome, and Francis of Assisi all accepted reincarnation. It was only rejected at the second Council of Constantinople in 553 CE, and then by a narrow vote. In more recent times, thinkers such as Weatherhead and C. S. Lewis have been open to it.[6] Among other so-called world religions, Buddhists and Hindus believe in it. It is often said that more people on earth believe in reincarnation than do not.

The World Wears Out

Even in the stricter sense of eschatology as the end of the world, there are strains of Native myth and belief that can be considered eschatological. Many Native American traditions, in fact, preserve such stories. More than five centuries of ongoing contact with Amer-Europeans and with Christianity have also led to what the late historian William McLoughlin termed "fractured myths," accounts reflecting a syncretism of traditional beliefs with Christian mythology, creating new, blended stories. Further, since Contact, there have arisen numerous messianic movements among Native peoples that look forward to the end of the world as we know it. According to Jace Weaver, "Such apocalyptic thinking, however, is only one part of a wider set of eschatological beliefs that long predate the advent of Europeans on this continent."[7]

Many tribes continue to tell stories that reflect what has been called "unrealized eschatological potential"—that is, myths in which it is possible, at least imaginatively, to contemplate the end of the world.[8] For example, the Tsimshian of the Northwest Coast believe that an Atlas-like strongman holds the world up on a hemlock pole. When the man shrugs or falters, earthquakes result. Should he collapse, the world will be destroyed, and all with perish. Similarly, the Winnebago are not to speak about their Medicine Rite "until the world comes to an end." There are even statements in the text of the ritual itself that the telling of the details will *cause* the end.

Most often this ending is seen as a natural event. It is viewed simply as a part of the order of the cosmos, the mirror image of creation. The world had a beginning, so it will have an end. The Lakota have a saying, "Only the rocks and mountains last forever." An example of such a natural conclusion is the Okanogan belief that, in the future, lakes will melt the foundation of the world, and rivers will cut it loose. The earth will float way, and that will be the end of the world.

Pre- and Post-Contact Eschatological Traditions

These are examples of unrealized eschatological potential. Numerous Native nations, however, have more developed eschatological traditions. It is often argued that such myths are post-Contact productions, reflecting exposure to Jewish and Christian myths concerning the eschaton. While it is impossible at this late date to say with absolute certainty whether they were part of Native cultures prior to the coming to Whites, the stronger case is that these stories *do* reflect pre-Contact traditions. Jace Weaver, who is the first to make such an argument and the foremost theorist of Native eschatological thought, bases this on a number of related considerations. First, very little, if anything, in many of these stories is indicative of a Christian or Amer-European worldview. Second, is it not likely that similar cultural thanatic fears and hopes for something better in the future would produce such stories in Native cultures as well as in those of the West? To put it a different way, very few contemporary scholars would claim that accounts of a deluge, present in many diverse world cultures throughout history, including Native American, were all derivative of the biblical story of Noah. Why then must it be assumed that all Native eschatological thinking is of Western origin? Finally, there is a marked difference between those accounts of last things that are most probably pre-Contact and those that are clearly post-Contact. This demonstrates a discernible change caused by the presence of the colonial invader and exposure to the invader's myths.[9]

Weaver groups pre-Contact stories into two broad categories. His categories overlap, and it is sometimes difficult to put a particular story into one group or the other. The first group is composed of what he terms "moral cautionary myths." The closest, though admittedly imperfect, analogies to stories in the biblical tradition might be to that of Noah and the Flood or, on a more localized scale, to the fate of Sodom and Gomorrah; in each God invokes destruction because of the irredeemable wickedness of humanity. The second set reflects traditional Native concepts of the cyclical, circular nature of time and reality. Weaver calls this category the "natural/cyclical."[10]

A Cheyenne belief is representative of the first group. According to the Cheyenne, there is a pole in the far north upon which the world rests. At its base sits a giant, snow-white beaver. Whenever humanity makes the beaver angry, it gnaws at the pole. When he chews through the last bit of the post, the world will crash, and it will be the end of everything. It is for this reason, according to Mrs. Medicine Bull, that the Cheyenne are careful not to anger the beaver, never eating its flesh or even touching its skin.

The second category is composed of those accounts in which there is a cycle of destruction and renewal. Such stories are familiar from the Maya, Aztec, and other Mesoamerican civilizations. There were numerous stories of world transformations at the passing of cyclical epochs. These eras passed in a great cataclysm followed by a re-genesis, a re-creation. The cycle was seen as continuous and was predicted for the future, as well as described as having occurred in the past.

Such thinking was natural to indigenous peoples who witnessed the cycles of the seasons with its endless circle of degeneration, death, and rebirth. The end of the world order, then, was seen in similar terms. Out of catastrophic destruction comes renewal. This mode of thinking can be seen in many North American tribes. The Lakota story of the old woman constantly weaving the destiny of the world, only to have her work repeatedly undone by her dog when her back is turned, is tied to the cycle of nature. Though not tied to the cycle of nature, a Chirachua Apache prophecy about the end time also envisions a "new world" after destruction.

Both pre-Contact strains of eschatology—the moral cautionary and the natural/cyclical—continue after European or Amer-European contact. Like much else about Native American life, however, they would be inevitably and forever changed by those events.

The Wintu of California have developed strong eschatological traditions since Contact. In 1941, Lucy Young related a prophecy of her grandfather. Before the coming of Whites, he had a dream in which White Rabbit devoured the Indian's grass, seed, and living. The man said, "We won't have nothing more, this world." Though scoffed at by his family, he predicted that his grandchildren would see it come to pass. Years before the publication of Young's story, Kate Luckie, a Wintu medicine woman, told an ethnographer, "When the Indians all die, then God will let the water come down from the north. Everyone will drown. That is because white people never cared for the land or deer or bear." Thus the moral cautionary warning to care for the rest of creation is linked with an implicit admonition to Whites to ensure Native survival.

In this century, many Native eschatological myths and prophecies have exhibited a distinct ecological cast. *The Zunis: Self-Portrayals*, published in 1972, contains a warning to humanity about the evils of alcohol, urban decay, overpopulation, and environmental devastation. The Hopi account of the destruction of the three previous worlds and the imminent destruction of this, the Fourth World, are now well known. This is due largely to the efforts of the Hopi themselves, who have disseminated the story, even speaking, at great effort, before the United Nations, and who have summoned the world to metanoia before it is too late. The prophecy predicts a period of *koyaanisquatsi*, or life out of balance, followed by a "Great Purification," after which the world will be reborn out of Hopiland. The story prediction probably has pre-Contact origins, fitting into a traditional pattern of destruction and renewal, the model of the natural/cyclical. Contact, however, and recent world events, including nuclear weapons, overpopulation, and ecological damage, have given the prophecy, if not new interpretations, at least a new urgency.

Messianic Traditions

Before examining the multiform answers to Jesus' question of Caesarea Philippi for Native cultures, it must be noted that there is a strain of messianic thought independent of Christianity. By "messianic" we mean a hoped for deliverer or leader—as Vine Deloria, Jr., puts it, a "radical intervention by God in history"—a divine savior figure whose advent somehow brings the present age to a close. There are messianic elements, for example, in the accounts of Quetzalcoatl of Mesoamerica, Degandawida and Hiawatha of the Iroquois, Pahana of the Hopi, in the Taki Onquoy (or Sickness Dance) of the Inca, and in historical leaders such as Popé of the Pueblo Revolt, Geronimo, Sweet Medicine, or Crazy Horse, among others. What sets these historical figures apart from Jesus, however, as Deloria points out, is that none of these cultural heroes ever "become the object of individual attention as to the efficacy of either the facts of their existence or of their present supertemporal ability to affect events."[11]

Though there are thus messianic elements in certain pre-Contact traditions, these become much more prominent after exposure to Christianity. Often these had a decidedly chiliastic aspect. The best known of these is the Ghost Dance movement in 1889-1890. It can be seen in a number of movements from the eighteenth century to the twentieth century. These movements are often known collectively as "ghost dance" movements. According to Weaver, however, it is better to reserve that appellation for the 1870 and 1889 Ghost Dances and to refer to the others as "raising up" movements (so-called because one of the salient features is the promise of the resurrection of dead friends and relatives).[12] It is worthwhile examining a few of such movements.

In 1762, a prophet named Neolin appeared among the Delaware, exhorting them to form a confederation of Indian nations to drive Whites back to the land from which they came. Natives were also to give up everything they had learned or received from Whites and to return to the old ways. The prophet stated that he had received this vision from the "Master of Life," who promised to give them success. In the hands of Pontiac, an Ottawa war leader, the prophecy led to a widespread Indian rebellion in the Great Lakes region.

In 1805, another prophet arose, this time among the Shawnee. Tenskwatawa, often called simply the Prophet, was the brother of Tecumseh. The Prophet claimed to have a new revelation from the Master of Life. The message was essentially the same as that received by the Delaware prophet. If Indians forsook White ways and drove Amer-Europeans from their territory, they would find favor. Game would return to their land and their dead would be restored to them. The Prophet was proclaimed to be the incarnation of Manabohzo, the Algonkian culture hero. His message received wide acceptance among Native nations and gained adherents from Florida to Saskatchewan, undergoing local variations as it went.

It was particularly effective among the Cherokee, where a medicine man named, according to Elias Boudionot, Tsali, and two others received visions of heavenly-sent Indians who warned that Corn Mother was angry with the Cherokee for abandoning her ways. He counseled a rejection of the White path; otherwise they would be destroyed. The prophet threatened to invoke a terrible storm, which would eradicate all but true believers in the new message. Another sign mentioned by the prophets was that the earth would shake and the Mississippi River would flow backwards. In 1811, the greatest earthquake ever to hit the North American continent struck on the New Madrid fault in Missouri. It was so powerful that it changed the course of the Mississippi and rang church bells in Baltimore, Maryland. According to Weaver, the story of the "removed townhouses," recorded by Mooney, probably dates from this period.[13]

Long before Removal, the Cherokee heard the voices of the Nûñnĕ´hĭ, the immortals who were like the Cherokee, only invisible, warning of all the wars and misfortunes that were to come. They invited the Cherokee to come live with them and gave them detailed instructions concerning what they must do if they were to do so. Two towns followed the instructions and were borne away. When the Cherokee were removed to Indian Territory, they had the deepest regret because they were forced to leave behind their relatives who had gone to Nûñnĕ´hĭ.[14]

In fact, many prophets arose among the Cherokee at this time. According to historian William McLoughlin, "Had the more immediate problem of war on their borders not forced attention to more mundane matters . . . this religious movement might have produced a single charismatic prophet who, like Tenskwatawa among the Shawnees or Handsome Lake among the Senecas, could have correlated all the feelings and half-articulated hopes and fears of the believers into a single, coherent, and compelling message around which the nation might have rallied. But no such prophet appeared. Many minor prophets rose and fell as their prophecies failed to materialize," and power eventually returned to secular leadership.[15]

The Apache have also experienced similar raising-up movements. In 1883, at Cibecue, following confinement on reservations, a medicine man with Lightning power, named Nakaidoklini, claimed to be able to raise the Apache dead to fight the Amer-Europeans. He was killed after a short-lived uprising before the movement could become widespread. From 1903 until 1907, the Apache experienced a movement called dahgodi•yáh' ("rising upwards" or "they will be raised up"). A Lightning medicine man again led it. Called Daslahdn, he had received a vision that he was to "lead the people up" into the sky after appropriate ceremonies. According to Jorge Noriega, there the people "would find a new world, and be free from the hatred, war and corruption of the old one," and "where wild fruits would be ripe all the time."[16] After the mysterious death of Daslahdn in 1906, the movement continued, spreading to the White Mountain Apaches from Cibecue; it dwindled by the following year. According to Noriega, the movement, though essentially traditionalist in origin, was the first to incorporate elements of both Apache and Christian religions.[17]

Numerous other syncretic religions contain distinctive messianic elements. Again, it is useful to review a few of these.

Following the American Revolution, a reformer arose among the Seneca. In 1799, Ganiodayo, or Handsome Lake, an alcohol-ridden old man, fell into a death trance and was guided on a Dantesque journey, presumably by Teharon-hiawagon, the primal being of life on earth. He emerged revived, preaching reform of the Iroquois religious traditions. The journey included a White inferno and a meeting with Jesus, whom he envisions as an eschatological messiah, who, rejected, has gone to bar the gates of heaven until his avenging return. Instead of a personal savior, however, Ganiodayo encounters Jesus as a fellow teacher, meeting him—to use biblical language—"face to face, as friend to friend."

Apropos of current theological debates concerning inculturation, it is important to note that Thomas Henry, in his book *Wilderness Messiah*, based on the unpublished papers of J. N. B. Hewitt, a Tuscarora in the employ of the Bureau of American Ethnology of the Smithsonian Institution, cautions, "Iroquois say that all accounts of the Handsome Lake religion written by white[s] are misleading and essentially meaningless, regardless of factual accuracy. Real understanding and appreciation, they insist, requires an Iroquois mind, for there are depths unfathomable by the white . . . mind."[18]

Among Natives of the Pacific Northwest, there is a syncretic religion with decidedly greater borrowings from Christianity. This is Tschaddam, or Indian Shaker religion. Having no relationship with the Christian sect of the same name, this is a revelatory, highly ritualized faith that considers itself a Christian denomination.

The church was founded by Squ-sacht-un (also known as John Slocum), a Squaxin, who either died or fell into a trance in 1881. He ascended to heaven where he was refused admittance because of his profligacy. Given the choice between going to hell or returning to earth and leading a righteous life and teaching others to do the same, he chose the latter.

Jesus occupies a leading place in Shakerism. He is affirmed as the offspring of God, a member of the Trinity, and the Savior of humankind. His passion is fully accepted. His ultimate judgment is expected, and such time will be a day of happiness and well-being when humanity will be healed. Shakers do not, however, accept the Bible as scripture. They believe that Slocum received direct revelation from Jesus Christ. The Bible is thus only history, an obsolete text for use only by Amer-Europeans.[19]

Among the Apache, a prophet known as Silas John rose to prominence in 1920 due to an increase in the number of "shooting witches" around the Fort Apache area. Dreams revealed to Silas John that many of the old medicine men were false and that a new world was imminent. He possessed both Lightning and Snake power, with the latter dominant. The primary symbol of the new faith was the cross with a snake. This symbol had the power to ward off witches and evil. Silas John himself was recognized as the reincarnation of Monster Slayer, the son of Changing Woman, the progenitor of all humanity. Monster Slayer was then identified in English with Jesus.[20]

The central themes of Silas John's movement continued from the earlier dahgodi•yáh'. People were to dance to be "raised up" into a new world free from the evil of this present one. In order to distinguish those who were to be raised from those left behind, followers were to wear a silver medal on their chests consisting of the cross and the crescent moon. Silas John also gave adherents new names. This was of crucial importance because, when the time of dahgodi•yáh' arrived, only those who remembered their new name would be saved.[21]

According to Noriega, the last published documentation of Silas John's movement dates to 1954. At that time, the prophet had been in prison for more than 20 years, but the dances were still being performed. Noriega notes, however, "The lasting effects of the Silas John movement are unknown outside Apache circles."[22]

The Ghost Dance that swept through Native communities

in the late nineteenth century began with a mystical vision of Jesus Christ by one Indian, Wovoka. It was an eschatological vision of Christ's parousia, a coming that would wipe Amer-Europeans off the face of the North American continent. After this righteous judgment, the dead would return, the buffalo would flourish, and all creation would be renewed. The movement had direct antecedents in the Ghost Dance of 1870 and in the Prophet Dance of Smohalla. Amer-European misunderstanding and fear of the Ghost Dance as a locus of political resistance led to the Wounded Knee massacre. The Ghost Dance, banned since the time of Wounded Knee, was revived in the 1970s by Henry Crow Dog and Leonard Crow Dog.

Vine Deloria once suggested that a Christian theology might be developed from the visions and thoughts of Black Elk, the Oglala Lakota holy man and seer. As Paul Steinmetz, a Jesuit who worked with the Oglala for many years, writes, "This [would fulfill] the Ghost Dance Messiah vision which Black Elk had in 1890. On later reflection, Black Elk recognized the Ghost Dance Messiah as Christ, which became the great mediating symbol between his conscious Catholic life and his repressed Lakota experience."[23] The historical contestation of Black Elk is far too complex to address here. He has been viewed variously as traditional holy man, Catholic catechist, and syncretic reformer.

By far the syncretic, messianic movement with the largest number of adherents is peyotism, which, in its various permutations accounts for approximately 25% of the Indian population in the United States. There are a number of peyotist sects and denominations, varying in the number of Christian elements they embrace. The principal problem in previous studies of them, as noted by Elizabeth Cook-Lynn, is "the continued definition of the religion as a *cult* and the persistence of the intellectual discussion of its features within that context."[24] The two primary rites within the Native American Church, the principal peyotist denomination, are the Half Moon way and the Cross Fire way.

In the Cross Fire way, the Bible is accepted, and water baptism is practiced. Jesus is accepted as Lord and Savior. His words are seen as eternal life, and there is healing through him. There is a strong emphasis on Christ's *parousia*, when there will be a judgment at which the good and bad of an individual will be weighed. Emerson Spider, Sr., a peyote roadman and a minister in the Church, refers to himself and others as "born-again Christians" and states, "The second coming of Christ is the only way to salvation." There is an emphasis on the atoning works of Christ; hymns used by the rite affirm that Christ died on the cross for our sins.[25] Spider wishes to merge the Native American Church more fully with Christian beliefs and desires recognition for it as a Christian denomination but acknowledges his views are not shared by all in the Church.

parousia

Asa Primeaux, Sr., explicitly criticizes Spider. Christ is not the only way. Recollecting the often abusive history of Christians toward Natives on this continent, he states, "[Y]ou'll never make me believe that Jesus Christ is the only one. No way. The Jesus Christ worshippers are nothing but murderers, idolaters, thieves." Jesus is not the mediator between humanity and God because no such mediation is necessary. Yet in some of Primeaux's songs, there is reference to both the Savior and a last day of judgment. They also speak of the pity of God and that the Savior alone has compassion.[26]

In the Half Moon way, the Bible is not present at meetings, but Jesus is neither denied nor ignored, and prayers normally end "in the name of Jesus. Amen." Christmas and Easter are celebrated with meetings. In practice, there is much interchange between the two rites, with persons often attending both. And although Jesus is de-emphasized in the Half Moon rite, it was at one such meeting that Vincent Catches, a Lakota, for instance, had a vision of Christ.[27]

Who Do You Say That I Am?

Within more orthodox Christian denominations, Natives have always had to answer Jesus' question of Caesarea Philippi for themselves. As we noted in the opening chapter, for all too many, the answer is that of fundamentalist Amer-European missionaries. Yet others have given more personal answers. Steven Charleston, the former Episcopal Bishop of Alaska and a Choctaw, has imaged Jesus' temptation in the wilderness as a vision quest. Aiban Wagua, a Kuna, has seen Jesus as the Indians massacred in the Conquest.[28] In a similar vein, Jack Forbes, Lenape/ Powhatan/ Saponi, has speculated that perhaps Jesus returned in Europe sometime between 300 and 1800 CE and was burned at the stake. He writes, "How many times have the Christians killed Jesus? Every time they murdered a 'heretic' or a heathen, every time they worked to death or starved to death a victim of their oppressive colonialism."[29] Elsa Tamez, who teaches at a seminary in San Jose, Costa Rica, relates Jesus to Quetzalcoatl.[30] Among certain Native peoples in Central America, Jesus is seen as the reincarnation of Quetzalcoatl.[31] In William Baldridge's story-based approach to theology, Jesus is primarily a teacher, who taught as the elders did that "good, not evil, is the most powerful enemy of the beast."[32] For Vine Deloria, Jr., Jesus is simply the eschatological prophet—the proclaimer who became the proclaimed.[33]

The issue of power cannot be overlooked. The syncretic faiths are wholly in the hands of Natives themselves to define. Among Native Christian congregations, those evidencing the highest degree of blending of traditional Indian and Christian practice and belief are generally those with Native leadership. The indigenous interpretations of Christ cited immediately previous are matters of individual conscience and interpretation. The late Audre Lorde declared, "The Master's tools will not dismantle his house." Hermeneuts like Asa Primeaux, Jack Forbes, and Vine Deloria remind us that it is a mistake to measure the master's house with the master's yardstick as well.

What then can be said about Native people and their answer to Jesus' question? Two predominant images emerge. The first is the triumphant, eschatological Christ. The other is the Suffering Jesus.

The eschatological Christ can be seen in the religion of

Handsome Lake and in the numerous raising-up movements, in particular the Ghost Dance movement of Wovoka. It can be seen in the emphasis on the parousia in peyotism. It can be seen in the equation of Jesus and Quetzalcoatl. It can be seen in the writing and preaching of William Apess, a Pequot and a Methodist, in the late 1820s and 1830s, who, while preaching Christ crucified and an inclusive *basileia*, nonetheless used Christianity not for assimilation but to assert his Indianness. He looked forward to "the day as not being far distant" when Christ would return, dispensing ample justice for all that has transpired between Whites and Natives.[34] Finally, the eschatological aspects are evident in the Passamaquoddy and Micmac myths concerning the departure and promised, apocalyptic return of Glooskap, discussed in our chapter on Trickster.

The other predominant image is that of the Suffering Jesus. Our experience of Native cultures leads us, along with many Natives, to find the doctrine of the atonement highly problematic. Instead, we concur with British theologians Leslie Weatherhead and W. R. Matthews, the latter of whom proclaimed, "We need to get clear on the point that no *doctrine* of the Atonement is part of the Christian Faith and that many different views are possible concerning the manner of Divine Foreigveness." As Jace Weaver writes, "I do not believe that Native communities, assaulted and deeply damaged by more than 500 years of colonialism, can believe that God in any way wanted or needed the death of Jesus on the cross to be 'reconciled' with humanity. Rather, many Natives aver that the crucifixion was the work of humanity and that when it occurred God wept. Then, however, as Psalm 2 states, God laughs with derision at the folly of humanity. God asks, 'Is that all there is? Is that the best you can do?' Then came, in response, the Resurrection."[35] The resurrection is God's resounding answer that evil and injustice will not have the last word. Like the triumphant, eschatological Christ, for Indians who continue to suffer oppression, the message of the resurrection, promising as it does ultimate justice, is an important one.[36]

Yet the Suffering Jesus remains important for many in our

community. Is this image severable from the crucified Jesus who provided an atoning sacrifice? As we have already indicated, we believe it is. Diane Glancy has written about the importance of the Suffering Jesus for her faith. She writes, "I see Christ standing on the prairie with his arms outstretched in love. A hole through his chest where his heart should be because this is what he lost when he was flesh in this world. When he was on earth, he was broken and fragmented like the Indian. . . . Terror must have devoured their hearts and limbs just as it must have Christ on the way to the cross."[37] For Cherokees, Jesus' march to Golgotha becomes the Trail of Tears when Cherokees sang a Christian hymn, asking, "Our heavenly father, what do I have to do for you to save me?" and answering "It only takes one drop of blood to wash away our sins."[38]

Reflecting Indian history, the importance of this Suffering Jesus, and the ritual-based nature of Native religious traditions, the Stations of the Cross have especial significance for many Native persons. Author Gerald Vizenor makes reference to this in his short story "The Baron of Patronia," when Novena Mae Ironmoccasin flees her boarding school, creating a wild Stations of the Cross on fourteen wounded trees before escaping into the woods.[39] In 1993, at a gathering of Native American seminarians, someone spoke of St. Paul's Chapel on the Navajo reservation where sandpaintings, tools of healing in Navajo religious traditions, make up the stations and spoke of God as "fellow sufferer," who knows what it is to be human.

Others, too, including Gustavo Gutiérrez (a Quechua), Aiban Wagua, and Elsa Tamez have written of the particular power of the Stations of the Cross for Native peoples in the Americas. For Wagua, it is a call to justice.[40] According to Gutiérrez, "The Way of the Cross is a choice made by free persons who reject death in all its forms: physical death, the death of egotistical sinfulness, and the death involved in disregarding and forgetting others."[41]

British theologian John Macquarrie writes, "Among other devotions, the one that perhaps most vividly encourages our active sharing in the life and ministry of our Lord is the one known as the Stations of the Cross, or the Way of the Cross. In this devotion, we walk with him along the way to Calvary."[42] Perhaps others participating in the ritual—non-Natives—can identify with Peter, or Simon of Cyrene, or Veronica, or even Pilate. But Indians, killed and deprived of their lands, especially those removed from their lands and subjected to genocidal reverse exoduses like the Trail of Tears or the Long Walk of the Navajo, cannot but identify with the Suffering Jesus. They can move imaginatively and viscerally into the racial memory of those treks. To borrow the words of Ernst Troeltsch, it becomes part of their own experience.

These then are but a few of the issues surfaced by a discussion of eschatology and messianism in Native thought and experience. Such a discussion touches on many considerations—identity, exclusivity, ecumenism, syncretism, atonement, salvation. True inculturation of the Christian faith among America's indigenous peoples has very little to do with pipes on altars, or church decorations, or "fulfillment theology," and everything to do with thought worlds and systems.[43]

AFTERWORD

N *ice place you got here—your country,*
my land.

E. Donald Two-Rivers[1]

In this volume, we have attempted to articulate a Native
American theology based upon the Native theological discourse that has blossomed in the past two decades. Such an ar-
ticulation is, as has been noted, only one of many possible ar-
ticulations. As we have also stated, we hope that this is only the
beginning of a new dialogue and that others will take up the
challenge after us. In setting forth this theology, we have employed many of the classic categories of Christian systematics
(e.g., creation, deity, theological anthropology, eschatology).
We have also included additional categories central to the experiences of Natives here on this continent, such as land and
trickster discourse. Throughout, we have kept the histories, religious traditions, and lived realities of Native peoples as our
central concern.

Traditional systematic theologies conclude with eschatology and ultimate salvation, with which we deal in the previous
chapter. We feel, however, that if our task is to be complete,
we must end with a discussion of current issues that face Native Americans as they live their lives in the twenty-first century. As Robert Warrior says in his book *Tribal Secrets*, "Our
struggle at the moment is to continue to survive and work toward a time when we can replace the need for being preoccu-
pied with survival with a more responsible and peaceful way of

living within communities and with the ever-changing landscape that will be our only home."[2] Though these contemporary concerns have informed all of our thinking and writing,
we believe that it is necessary to conclude with a more explicit
explication of them.

Racism

Several years ago, in an essay for English class, a Minnesota
ninth grader called Native Americans "beer-bellied poaching
maniacs." He wrote, "They think that because they were in
America before we were, they should be able to kill as many of
whatever kind of animal they wish. But as I recall, we won the
country fair and square. We are a dying race. They are expand-
ing like rabbits, and soon we will be the minority and live by
their laws." In the upper Midwest, a region where Native
hunting and fishing rights guaranteed by treaty have led to
sometimes violent clashes—"Spear an Indian; save a walleye"
and "Spear a pregnant squaw; save two walleye" are common
slogans—the paper caused a brief stir and then was quickly
forgotten.

Today the expression of such attitudes probably does not
surprise the majority of Amer-Europeans any longer. White
supremacists and militia groups of the self-declared "patriot
movement" regularly give voice to similar views about Indians
and other people of color, their speech protected by a founding
document of the culture and government they claim to de-
spise. But as one Native American professor asked, "If Indians
and Blacks went out in the woods and started drilling with
guns, how long do you think *that* would last?" The opinions of
the fourteen-year-old in his school essay, undoubtedly learned
from his parents, would *never* have surprised a Native American. They only illustrate what Natives have been saying all
along—racism against America's indigenous peoples remains
real and pervasive.

Creek poet Joy Harjo, in her poem "Anchorage," points out

the irony of Native Americans in the twenty-first century—
"those who were never meant . . . to survive." In a similar vein,
Cherokee writer Thomas King has called the continuance of
Natives one of "life's little embarrassments" for the dominant
culture. Yet, despite all expectations to the contrary, they have
survived. It may be, as Robert Warrior terms it, "the fragile
miracle of survival," but it is survival nonetheless. And it is not
simply the survival of individualized, assimilated Natives—the
hoped-for product of Richard Henry Pratt's educational philosophy, "Kill the Indian to save the man." Instead, Natives
have survived as communities and as tribes to claim the rights
and sovereignty guaranteed to them by treaty, the United
States Constitution, and international law.

It is this assertion of rights that has once again made Natives—and racism against them—visible in America. David
Larsen, a psychologist and a Dakota, attributes much of the
racism against Natives to unresolved anger on the part of
Amer-Europeans. According to him, settlers were often mis-
led about the land they were moving to occupy: "They were
told the land was free, that nobody owned it, and they could
just come and take it. They weren't mean. They believed what
they were told. And all of a sudden there were people like us
saying, 'No, you can't have this. This is ours. And we're not
going to change.' They thought we were making it up." While
not all Natives would subscribe to Larsen's benign estimation
of Amer-European motives, there is no gainsaying an element
of truth in his analysis.

Most Amer-Europeans continue to be amazed at this survival of Native Americans as distinct cultures and groups.
Many Whites grew up believing that Indians died out in the
nineteenth century. Once in awhile they would see modern-
day Natives and merely dismiss them as colorful relics of a fast-
receding and evermore distant past. One oddly common view
held by Whites is that Native Americans have an opportunity
not available to African Americans or Asian Americans or
many other ethnic minorities: they can simply give up their
culture and "become White." Amer-Europeans, raised on the

image of the United States as a great melting pot, do not understand why Natives would not want to take advantage of such an "opportunity."

Natives stand as a sore reminder of a conquest that is still contested and not quite complete. The resurgence of Native American identity and sovereignty is viewed by many as a claim for "special rights." The impressions of a Minnesota teenager notwithstanding, it is unlikely that Natives, who today make up less than one percent of the U.S. population, will be able to exercise enough power electorally to be much of a force. Even so, the unexpected endurance of Natives and the "nations-within-a-nation" status of tribes, inconsistent and ever-changing federal policies, and the persistence of nineteenth-century attitudes on the part of many Whites have led to a number of other issues for contemporary Natives as they enter the twenty-first century.

Land Claims

The fundamental issue affecting the relationship between Natives and Amer-Europeans can never be rectified because it has to do with the land itself and the manner in which it was wrested from the hundreds of individual tribes throughout the continent. It is an issue unique to Indian peoples since, among all peoples in the United States, only they are indigenous to this place. Consequently, in current disputes over land and resources (e.g., uranium, coal, water, timber), even other ethnic groups are seldom active in the support of Natives.

Racism and resentment toward Native Americans also has been fueled by a few notable, if incomplete, successes in asserting land claims. In 1980, Congress passed the Maine Indian Claims Settlement Act, awarding three tribes (Passamaquoddy, Penobscot, and Houlton Band of Maliseet) $81.5 million in settlement of their land claims. Subsequently, the tribes used approximately $54.5 million to purchase 305,000 acres of land in the state. That same year, the Supreme Court ruled that the Black Hills had been taken illegally from the Sioux, awarding them $100 million. The decision demonstrated the fundamental difference between Native cultures on the one hand and Western, Amer-European culture on the other. The only remedy in Amer-European courts for the taking was monetary compensation. The only remedy that interested the Lakota was restoration of the land. Twenty years later, the money remains unclaimed.

Adding credence to Larsen's theory about unresolved anger, many Amer-Europeans, while acknowledging wrongs in the past, see the dispossession of Natives as simply that—past. It happened long ago, and they, such individuals will say, had nothing to do with it. Even so, a number of Christian denominations have issued apologies to Native Americans. Such stances fail to recognize that the taking of Native lands is an ongoing theft. Speaking of apartheid in South Africa, Archbishop Desmond Tutu said, "If you take my pen, what good does an apology do, if you still keep my pen?"

Today, only the most winsome dreamer or the most visionary prophet believes that Amer-Europeans are going anywhere—short of the success of the Ghost Dance or cataclysmic destruction brought upon themselves (which destruction would probably take Indians along, too). We must find a way to co-exist on this continent which we now involuntarily share. To continue to resist just Native land claims and refuse reparations as compensation for lands illegally taken is to engage in an unhealthy and dangerous psychological denial about the conquest of this continent and the nature of our cohabitation on it.

Stereotyping

Today, if asked what their images of Native Americans are, most people would respond with a variety of pictures from pulp novels, movies, or television. Almost all these representations have been produced by non-Natives. The result is that

Native Americans remain the one racial/ethnic minority that non-Natives, even those who would be sympathetic to Native causes and issues, will not let move into the twentieth—let alone the twenty-first—century. In their mind's eye, they still imagine "real" Indians living in teepees and hunting buffalo from dappled ponies. Anything or anyone who does not fit this romantic stereotype is labeled as inauthentic. In fact, in the 1950s and 1960s, influential publisher Henry Luce barred coverage of Native Americans in *Time* and *Life*, contending that modern Natives were "phonies."

The stereotype, like all stereotypes, is almost a complete fabrication. To the extent that it has any basis in reality, it depicts the Plains Indians of the nineteenth century. It fails to take into account the incredible diversity among Native nations and the change over time that occurs in any living culture.

Even so, non-Natives expect modern-day Native Americans to "look Indian"—that is to say, to fit the stereotype. Several years ago, one prominent Native novelist and college professor was even asked before a radio interview if he could "sound Indian"! Even well-meaning non-Natives will ask Indians questions such as, "Did you grow up on a reservation?" or "Do you play the drum?" Such questions are offensive to many Native Americans and reflect a continued ignorance about the lives of contemporary Indians.

Wannabes

According to the 1990 census, there are almost two million Native Americans living in the United States. This figure, however, is problematic for several reasons. First, many Natives contend, with justification, that their numbers are significantly undercounted by the census. On the other hand, the census relies on self-identification. A number of persons included in the count are simply "census Indians" or "box checkers," persons who may or may not have Native American ancestry but who are not tribal members and have no ties to a

Native community. To Native Americans, such persons are "wannabes." They point at some vague, distant ancestor who was Indian and will generally describe themselves as "part Indian." Most times they display little or no knowledge of, or interest in, Native Americans or their affairs. Although a certain number of persons throughout history have posed as Indians, the problem has increased in recent years as movies such as *Dances with Wolves* and the impression that all Indians are rich from casino gambling have combined to make Indians "chic."

Often Indians find these "wannabes" amusing, considering them to be harmless and silly. Such poseurs, as well as the phenomenon that produces them, actually contribute, however, to increased racism against Natives. These persons are in reality part of the dominant culture. Their existence adds to pressure for assimilation of "other" Native Americans. They create an atmosphere in which it seems nearly all Americans are "part Indian," thus diluting the impact when Native nations attempt to claim their rights. They also obscure the fact that many real Native Americans, for a variety of historical reasons, are not members of any federally recognized tribe. The historic and continuing intrusion of the federal government into questions of Indian identity adds to the confusion.

As a result, old misconceptions and nineteenth-century stereotypes are perpetuated. Indians are subjected to a subtle form of racism from which other racial and ethnic minorities are exempt. They are routinely asked, "How much Indian are you?" or "Are you a mixed blood?" They are then categorized based upon their answers. Those who insist that inquiries into "blood quantum" are not racially motivated and that they have nothing to do with whether the person before them fits their stereotypical view of what is an "Indian" must ask themselves a question: would they ever consider asking an African American, no matter how light-skinned, "Are you a half-breed Black?" or "How much African are you?" Such questions are as offensive to Native Americans as they would be to African Americans or any other person. The simplest answer to persons who ask such questions is that Indians do not come in "parts." Birth, tribal membership, culture, and practice determine who is Indian. One is either Indian or one is not.

Mascots, Brand Names, and Cultural Appropriation

Americans' fascination with Indians creates other issues as well. Popular culture has thoroughly exploited the stereotypes of Indians in movies and books and on television. There are, however, other uses to which images of Indians are put by the dominant culture. Sports teams and products are merchandised using Indian names. All across the country, people can root for football or baseball teams with names like "Indians," "Braves," "Scouts," "Warriors," or even "Redskins." They can drive to and from their games in their Pontiacs, Dakotas, and Cherokees. Until recently, they could toast the victory with a frosty glass of Crazy Horse Malt Liquor. When Natives protest the use of such terms, they are usually viewed as overly sensitive cranks complaining about trivial matters. These names, it is often claimed, are meant to honor Indians. They are, however, emblems of a racist past and, as such, are offensive to many Natives. It is hard to convey precisely the implications of these things and the depth of the insult felt by many Indians. Imagine a beer, marketed specifically at African Americans, labeled "Malcolm Xport" or a breath candy for Asian Americans called "Sun Yat Sen-Sen." Would these names be seen as "honoring" the contribution of ethnic minorities?

A far more serious problem exists in the appropriation and practice of Native religious traditions by non-Natives. With the rise of environmental consciousness and the New Age movement, Americans' continuing fascination with Indians has attracted many to Native "spirituality." Non-Native practice of Indian religious traditions is objectionable to many Native Americans, who recall that the practice by Natives themselves was banned until 1934 (and until the 1950s in Canada) and see the new attraction as a mark of colonialism. Typical of the view of New Age adherents of Native spirituality is that of

Gary Snyder, a non-Native poet and self-proclaimed "sha-man." Snyder states that religion cannot be "owned," contending, "In this sense, it seems to me that I have as much right to pursue and articulate the belief systems developed by Native Americans as they do, and arguments to the contrary strike me as absurd in the extreme." By contrast, Native Americans often see the issue as exactly one of ownership. They see appropriation as an attempt by Amer-Europeans, whose ancestors conquered this continent, to "own" the heritage of Natives as thoroughly as they claim to own the land and its resources. Russell Means put the matter starkly when he named it a problem "because spirituality is the basis of our culture; if it is stolen, our culture will be dissolved. If our culture is dissolved, Indian people as such will cease to exist."

These persons who want to experience and practice Native spirituality may in reality have nothing to do with Native Americans. They often know little or nothing about Native American history or contemporary Indians. They do not want to commit themselves to the justice struggles of Indians. They do not want anything to damage their romantic notions of stereotyped Indians and their religious practices.

Local bookstores are flooded with volumes on Native "spirituality." Many of these, even some written by supposed Indians, are frauds. Sincere, unsuspecting Amer-Europeans buy books by Lynn Andrews, Jamake Highwater, or Dhyani Ywahoo (to name only a few examples), believing that they are getting legitimate information about Indians. Instead, they are getting homogenized or even wholly fictive "tradition" that has little or nothing to do with authentic Indians and their practices. They are left confused, bewildered, and often angry, about what is genuine and what is not.

Native women continue to struggle with the feminist movement. In their struggles for their own rights as Native women, they are often divided on whether to ally themselves with other feminists. Some choose to do so. Others contend that feminism is more concerned with issues that are important to middle-class White women rather than to women of color and see among Amer-European feminists many of the same people in-volved in New Age appropriation of Native religious tradi-tions. Native women even remain divided on the use of the word "feminist." While some use it to describe themselves, others prefer the term "womanist," coined by African Ameri-can women as a more inclusive term that better describes their brand of activism.

Freedom of Religion and Its Violation

Though Native religious traditions have been subject to consumption by hungry non-Natives at the "spiritual delica-tessen" ("Give me a slice of sweat lodge and a piece of vision quest with mayonnaise on fry bread"), freedom of religion re-mains elusive for Native Americans themselves. Native reli-gious traditions are threatened by the destruction of sacred sites due to development and by laws that make traditional cer-emonies difficult. Although freedom of religion is supposedly guaranteed to Natives by the First Amendment and the Indian Civil Rights Act of 1968, Congress felt compelled to affirm that guarantee in the American Indian Religious Freedom Act of 1978 ("AIRFA"). But the United States Supreme Court, in two major cases—*Lyng v. Northwest Indian Cemetery Protective Association* in 1988 and *Employment Division v. Smith* in 1990—rendered that act useless and showed the Court's scant appreci-ation of Native religious traditions.

After AIRFA proved ineffective, Congress attempted in 1993 to protect religious freedom again in two bills, the Reli-gious Freedom Restoration Act and the Native American Free Exercise of Religion Act, designed, among other things, to undo the damage of the *Lyng* and *Smith* decisions. In 1997, however, the Supreme Court declared the former act unconsti-tutional, and the latter would seem open to challenge. Thus, in the words of the late Justice Harry Blackmun in his dissent in *Smith*, freedom of religion remains "merely an unfulfilled and hollow promise."

Even Native American cultural and sacred objects and human remains of Natives themselves have not been safe from violation. During the nineteenth and twentieth centuries, thousands of Indian cultural and ceremonial objects were taken and placed in museums. Skeletons of Native Americans were also shipped to museums for display and "scientific study." In a macabre joke, it was said that the Smithsonian Institutution in Washington had more dead Indians in its collection than there were live Indians. In 1990, in response to protests by Native American groups, Congress enacted the Native American Graves Protection and Repatriation Act, requiring the return of human remains and cultural and religious objects to Native nations. The act, however, has been unpopular with museums, which have been slow to comply, and it has been at the center of a highly-charged court case involving rights to a 9,400-year-old skeleton discovered on the Washington-Oregon border in 1996.

Native Americans and the Church

History records countless incidents in which the European-descended peoples have pitted race against race, ethnic against ethnic, and have even used individuals within a particular group against their own people in order to achieve their goals of suppressing these groups and taking their resources. The Church was not an exception when it came to the nitty gritty of land grabbing on the part of Amer-Europeans. Alexander Talley, a Methodist missionary used his influence to remove Choctaws to Indian Territory, precipitating the infamous "Trail of Tears," which resulted in the death of a quarter of the population of the Five Civilized Tribes in the 1830s. Col. John Chivington was a Methodist clergyman who led the Colorado militia in the Sand Creek Massacre in which Black Kettle's band of peaceful Cheyenne were slaughtered and mutilated. It was missionaries of all denominations who pressed the U.S. government to promulgate the so-called "Religious Crimes

Codes," forbidding practice of Native religious traditions.

The destruction of Native religious traditions was mandated because, according to former Commissioner of Indian Affairs John Collier, "the religions made the tribes strong, and made the individuals of the tribe immune to intimidation or corruption." Christian missionaries were committed to the task of undermining Native cultures regardless of the means used to do so. Elkanah Walker, a missionary in Oregon Territory described the process in a letter, "It seems the only [way] they can be saved from being destroyed from the face of the earth is by their yielding to the control of the whites, and nothing will induce them to do this but a cordial reception of the gospel, and how can this be done without the labors of a christian [sic] missionary."

In 1910, the Bureau of Indian Affairs published a report which graded various Native tribes on their level of acculturation. Those tribes who had given up most of their culture (on a percentage scale of 1-100) were designated "well advanced." Those who retained 50% or so of their culture (however measured) were labeled "fairly advanced." Those who retained most or all of their culture were labeled "little advanced." The term "advanced" is clearly an Amer-European cultural judgment and illustrates the bigotry that has gotten in the way of efforts to understand the Native American situation. The result of such degrading estimates by churches and government agencies has often been reflected in the remarks of missionized Indians. At one time a pamphlet was circulated in the Mississippi Annual Conference of the United Methodist Church, allegedly written by a Choctaw convert. It declares, "Born as I was in that dark heathen world, I was a savage. I knew nothing of the true God but like all intelligent creatures I desired to worship something outside of self and so I worshipped an undefinable 'Great Spirit' whose voice was heard in the purling brooks and the soughing pines that bordered the forest. I grew to manhood among a people who had no schools, who had no bible [sic], who had no Christ and who, therefore, had no hope save in the paleface who could give us the blessings of civilization." Thus the goal of many missionaries seemed to be to convince Native Americans that there was neither hope nor future in Native traditions, that they were totally depraved both culturally and spiritually, and that the solution was to submit to reconditioning in the Amer-European cultural system. Some Native Americans have accepted that analysis and become missionized. The majority rejected the premise. Some accepted the analysis but rejected the solution.

The alienation of Native Americans from Christianity, however, is caused by more than history. In many locations, denominations still too often confuse Christianity with their own Amer-European culture and values. They will not allow Indians to be Indians. Even after 500 years, Natives are still taught that to become Christian means to stop being Indian. Vine Deloria illustrated perhaps the height of this attitude several years ago when he told of his encounter with a Presbyterian missionary who had worked with the Shinnecock on New York's Long Island. Deloria inquired how long the man's denomination intended to continue mission operations to a tribe that had lived as a Christian community for 350 years. The man replied simply, "Until the job is done."

Poverty and Other Issues

The reality for most Native Americans stands in stark contrast to the romantic notions of Indians held by many in the dominant culture. Today, Indians remain indisputably an oppressed minority in the United States. "The result," writes sociologist Menno Boldt in his book *Surviving as Indians*, "is a cultural crisis manifested by a breakdown of social order in Indian communities." The often-repeated statistics are staggering. The average yearly income is less than half the poverty level, and over half of all Natives are unemployed. On some reservations, unemployment runs as high as 85-90%. Health statistics chronically rank Native Americans at or near the bottom. Male life expectancy is 44 years, female 47. Infant mortality is twice the national average. Diabetes runs six times the national average; heart disease at about five times the national average; alcoholism five times the national average; and cirrhosis of the liver 18 times the national average. Substance abuse, school dropout rates, suicide, crime, and violence are major problems among both urban and reservation populations. Increasingly, violence victimizes those with least power— women, children, the elderly. Though Native Americans may often be, to the untrained eye, indistinguishable from the population at large, they still go to jail in disproportionate numbers, earn less, and die younger.

Casino gaming on reservations has brought prosperity to a few tribes. They have used the proceeds for economic development, cultural preservation, housing, education, and healthcare. They have also used funds generated to repurchase their land base, creating friction with their non-Native neighbors. While such uses are laudable, the statistics cited above show that gaming has hardly been a cure-all. The issue has divided many Native nations, and though gaming has again made Native Americans "visible" to the majority of Americans, it has also led to renewed assaults on tribal sovereignty. Measures have been introduced in Congress to strip tribal nations of their sovereign immunity, for instance. Also, a recent book has, in smear-job fashion, attacked the Mashantucket Pequot, the most successful gaming tribe, claiming they are not, in fact, entitled to federal recognition and calling for a congressional investigation.

Today, more than 2/3 of Native Americans live in cities, removed from traditional lands and cultures. These Indians are America's most invisible minority. They walk city streets and ride buses or trains unseen next to other urban dwellers. If they are noticed at all, they are mistaken by non-Natives for Hispanic, Asian, Jewish, or Italian. This invisibility has led many urban natives to become the invented Indian of popular imagination. They wear long hair, beads, and "Indian dress," because not to play the invention game is to risk becoming invisible.

Meanwhile, civil unrest in Mexico and Central America has caused a large influx of Natives into the United States. It has swelled Indian populations, particularly in cities. The most spoken Indian language in the United States is now Zapoteca. Significantly, the tracks of this migration often cross reservations. These new indigenous immigrants have brought about increased cultural interchange, helped strengthen a hemispheric consciousness among Natives, and led to new constellations of identity.

Conclusion

These issues, related but separate, in addition to many others referenced in this work, profoundly affect any Native theology. It is for this reason that we chose to conclude on this, what might seem to be a negative—even sour—note, having little to do with theology. But, though not necessarily couched in traditional theological language, the upshot of these matters is very much theological.

Today, Native nations work to maintain their cultures and languages in the face of continued pressure to assimilate. As they have since the first coming of Europeans more than five centuries ago, Native Americans struggle, in the words of a young Cree essayist, Murray Stonechild, to survive as Indians, to know who they are as persons, and to maintain their "soul selves." They continue their resistance. They remain true warriors.

NOTES

Introduction

1. Leslie Silko, *Ceremony* (New York: New American Library, 1977) 1. Thought Woman is the creative force in Laguna cosmology.

2. U.S. Bureau of the Census, *1990 Census of Population: Social and Economic Characteristics: American Indian and Alaska Native Areas* (Washington, DC: U.S. Government Printing Office, 1993); Indian Health Service, U.S. Department of Health and Human Services, *Trends in Indian Health* (Washington, DC: U.S. Government Printing Office, 1995). We know enough about the 2000 census at this time to say that the statistics will not shift dramatically in any category for Native Americans. Glenn Morris, "International Law and Politics: Toward a Right to Self-Determination for Indigenous Peoples," in M. Annette Jaimes, *The State of Native America* (Boston: South End, 1992), 71, 84n. See also Tinker and Loring Bush, "Statistical Games and Cover-ups: Native American Unemployment," in George Shepherd and David Penna, *Racism and the Underclass in America* (Greenwood Press, 1991) 119-44.

3. William Apess, *On Our Own Ground: The Complete Writings of William Apess, a Pequot*, ed. Barry O'Connell (Amherst: The University of Massachusetts Press, 1992) xiii.

4. James Axtell, *The Invasion Within: The Contest of Cultures in Colonial North America* (New York: Oxford University Press, 1985) 131-78.

5. Francis Jennings, *Invasion of America* (Chapel Hill, NC: The University of North Carolina Press, 1975) 238-39, 251-52.

6. Elaine Pagels, *Adam, Eve, and the Serpent* (New York: Vintage Books, 1989) 15-16.

7. Roy Harvey Pearce, *Savagism and Civilization: A Study of the Indian and the American Mind* (Baltimore: The Johns Hopkins University Press, 1964) 19.

8. James Axtell, *The European and the Indian* (Oxford: Oxford University Press, 1981) 270.

9. 3 *U.S. Statutes at Large 85* (1819).

10. Anthony F. C. Wallace, "Revitalization Movements," *American Anthropologist* 58 (1956) 264-82.

11. Edward Spicer, "European Expansion and the Enslavement of Southwestern Indians," *Arizona and the West*, I (Summer 1959) 132; Edward H.

Spicer, *Cycles of Conquest: The Impact of Spain, Mexico, and the United States on the Indians of the Southwest, 1533-1960* (Tucson: The University of Arizona Press, 1962) 503-504.

12. *Principles for Inculturation of the Catechism of the Catholic Church* (Department of Education, United States Catholic Conference, 1994) 1.

13. Edward H. Spicer, "Yaqui," in *Perspectives in American Indian Culture Change* (Chicago: The University of Chicago Press, 1961) 58-60.

14. Edward H. Spicer, *Cycles of Conquest: The Impact of Spain, Mexico, and the United States on the Indians of the Southwest 1533-1960* (Tucson: The University of Arizona Press, 1962) 192-93.

15. Tinker, "Religion," in *Encyclopedia of North American Indians: Native American History, Culture, and Life from Pleo-Indians to the Present*, ed. Frederick E. Hoxie (New York: Houghton Mifflin, 1996) 537-38.

16. See the suggestive but all-too-short comment in Engelbert Mveng, "African Theology," in *Voices from the Third World*, vol. 18, no. 1 (June 1995) 114-15.

17. M. Annette Jaimes and Theresa Halsey, "American Indian Women," in Jaimes, *The State of Native America: Genocide, Colonization and Resistance* (Boston: South End Press, 1992) 311-44.

18. In a public lecture by George Tinker at the Claremont School of Theology in August, 1994.

19. Gary Witherspoon, *Language and Art in the Navajo Universe* (Ann Arbor: University of Michigan Press, 1977) 25.

20. Keith Basso, *Wisdom Sits in Places: Landscape and Language Among the Western Apache* (Albuquerque: University of New Mexico Press, 1996) 56-57.

1. Hermeneutics

1. *The New Bible Dictionary*, ed. F. F. Bruce, et al. (Grand Rapids: Eerdmans, 1962) 992.

2. Joseph T. Shipley, *Dictionary of Word Origins*, 2nd ed. (New York: Philosophical Library, [1945]) 180.

3. Karlfriend Froehlich, *Biblical Interpretation in the Early Church* (Philadelphia: Fortress Press, 1984) 28.

4. *The Westminster Dictionary of Christian Theology* (Philadelphia: Westminster Press, 1983) 253.

5. Friedrich Schleiermacher, *Hermeneutics and Criticism*, trans. and ed. Andrew Bowie (Cambridge: Cambridge University Press, 1998) 127.

6. Calvin Martin, *Keepers of the Game: Indian-Animal Relationships and the Fur Trade* (Berkeley: University of California Press, 1978) 145-46.

7. Richard A. Horsley, *Bandits, Prophets and Messiahs* (Philadelphia: Trinity Press, 1999). Using Jewish Palestine as an example, he states that in any traditional society "The peasantry comprise 90% of the population."

8. Ibid.

9. Arthur H. with George McPeek, *The Grieving Indian* (Winnipeg: Intertribal Christian Communications, 1988).

10. Helmut Thielicke, *Nihilism: Its Origin and Nature—with a Christian Answer* (New York: Harper Brothers Publisher, 1961) 9.

11. Ibid., 21.

12. Richard Henry Pratt, *Battlefield and Classroom: Four Decades with the American Indian, 1867-1904*, ed. Robert M. Utley (Lincoln, NE: University of Nebraska Press, 1964) 260.

2. Creation

1. Tink Tinker took primary responsibility for this chapter.

2. Edmund Nequatewa, *Truth of a Hopi* (Flagstaff, AZ: Museum of Northern Arizona, 1967) 33.

3. Percy Bullchild, *The Sun Came Down: The History of the World as My Blackfeet Elders Told It* (San Francisco: Harper and Row, 1985) 5-6.

4. Richard Erdoes and Alfonso Ortiz, eds., *American Indian Myths and Legends* (Pantheon, 1984) 46-47. Alfonso Ortiz, *Tewa World: On Time, Space, Being, and Becoming in a Pueblo Society* (Chicago: University of Chicago Press, 1969) 13-14. Elsie Clews Parsons, *Pueblo Indian Religion*, 2 vols. (Chicago: University of Chicago Press, 1939) 210-66.

5. See Arthur C. Parker, *Seneca Myths and Folk Tales*, Buffalo Historical Society Publications 27 (1923) 59-73; for an Onandoga version, see J. N. B. Hewitt (Tuscarora), *Iroquoian Cosmology—Second Part*, Annual Report of the Bureau of American Ethnography 43 (1928) 479-87. Both versions are reprinted, in edited form, in Elizabeth Tooker, *Native North American Spirituality of the Eastern Woodlands* (New York: Paulist Press, 1979) 35-55.

6. The Osage descent was also to a world inundated with water. In the Osage version, a mystical elk (O-po^n to^n-ga) separated the earth and the waters. The hairs of its hide provided the earth with grasses and with other plants for food. See Francis LaFlesche, "The Osage Tribe: Rite of the Chiefs; Sayings of the Ancient Men," *Thirty-Sixth Annual Report of the Bureau of American Ethnography* (1914-15), Washington, D.C.: U. S. Government Printing Office, 1921, 165-66.

7. John Joseph Matthews, *The Osages: Children of the Middle Waters* (Norman, OK: University of Oklahoma Press, 1961) 3-19.

8. Kirkpatrick Sale, *The Conquest of Paradise: Christopher Columbus and the Columbian Legacy* (New York: Albert A. Knopf, 1990) 74-91. Also, Thomas Berry, *Dance of the Earth* (Sierra Club, 1988); Carolyn Merchant, *The Death of Nature* (Harper, 1981); Lawrence D. Roberts, ed., *Approaches to Nature in the Middle Ages*, Center for Medieval and Early Renaissance Studies (SUNY, Binghampton, 1982).

9. Sale, 82.

10. See Francis La Flesche, *The War and Peace Ceremony of the Osage Indians*, Bureau of American Ethnography, Bulletin 101 (1939).

11. Leslie Silko's famous novel, *Ceremony* (New York: Viking, 1977), is precisely about such a situation. The novel deals with the healing and cleansing of a World War II veteran for whom a new ceremony had to be devised. Social and spiritual complexities of disintegration and alienation had made it

much more difficult for the Laguna people and for himself. Thus, his healing has to do with the healing of the whole community and not just of himself.

12. Vine Deloria, Jr., *God Is Red: A Native View of Religion* (Golden, CO: North American Press, 1992, revised [1972]).

13. Tinker, "Spirituality and Native American Personhood; Sovereignty and Solidarity," in *Spirituality of the Third World*, edited by K.C. Abraham and Bernadette Mbuy-Beya (Maryknoll, NY: Orbis Books, 1994) 119-32; "An American Indian Reading of the Bible," in *New Interpreter's Bible*, ed. Leander E. Keck, et al. (Nashville: Abingdon, 1994) 174-80; and "Native Americans and the Land: The End of Living and the Beginning of Survival," *Word and World* 6 (1986) 66-75.

14. Proverbs 8:22-31 offers a very different story of creation than either of the Genesis chapters.

3. Deity

1. Åke Hultkranz, *The Religions of American Indians* (University of California, 1967); "The Structure of Theistic Beliefs among North American Plains Indians," in *Belief and Worship in Native North America* (Syracuse University Press, 1981) 20-27.

2. Paul Radin, "Religion of the North American Indians," *Journal of American Folklore* 27 (1914) 335-73; Jordan Paper, "The Post-Contact Origin of an American Indian High God: The Suppression of Feminine Spirituality," *American Indian Quarterly* 7 no. 4 (1983) 1-21; Hultkranz, "The Concept of the High God," in *The Religions of the American Indians*, 15-26.

3. Ruth Benedict, "Religion," in *General Anthropology*, ed. Franz Boas (Boston: D.C. Heath and Sons, 1932) 627-65.

4. J. N. B. Hewitt, "Orenda and a Definition of Religion," *American Anthropologist* 4 (1902) 33-46; William Jones, "The Algonkin Manitou," *Journal of American Folklore* 18 (1905) 183-90; Alice Fletcher, "Wakonda," in *Handbook of American Indians*, vol. 2 (Bureau of American Ethnology, Bulletin 30); "Wakondagi," *American Anthropologist* 14 (1912) 106-109; Radin, "Religion of the North American Indians," *Journal of American Folklore* 27 (1914) 335-73; Elizabeth Tooker, *Native North American Spirituality of the Eastern Woodlands* (Paulist Press, 1979) 11-30.

5. Hultkranz, "The Supernatural," in *The Religions of the American Indians* 9-14; Benedict, 631.

6. See Walker's 1912 letter to Clark Wissler at the American Museum of Natural History, quoted in Elaine A. Jahner, ed., *Lakota Myth* (Lincoln, NE: University of Nebraska Press, 1983) 8: "Some would give one portion of the mythology and others other parts, which, if I had not known something of the matter would have been very confusing and this did confuse me for many years. There are some contradictions in the mythology, especially in appellations as for instance, the Rock who is the Grandfather while the sun is often addressed as Grandfather."

7. Sam D. Gill, *Mother Earth: An American Story* (Chicago: University of Chicago Press, 1987) 8.

8. See, for example, Elsie Clews Parsons, *Pueblo Indian Religion*, 2 vols. (Chicago: University of Chicago Press, 1939).

9. See Francis LaFlesche, "The Osage Tribe: Rite of the Chiefs," *Thirty-sixth Annual Report of the Bureau of American Ethnology, 1914-15* (Washington, D.C.: U.S. Government Printing Office, 1921) 69.

10. James Owen Dorsey, "Osage Traditions," *Sixth Annual Report of the Bureau of Ethnology, 1884-85* (Washington, D.C.: U.S. Government Printing Office, 1888) 396.

11. James Owen Dorsey, "Siouan Sociology," *Fifteenth Annual Report of the Bureau of Ethnology* (Washington, D.C.: U.S. Government Printing Office, 1897) 205-44.

12. In Paul Radin, *Die religiöse Erfahrung der Naturvölker* (Zurich: Rhein-Verlag, 1951).

13. David Bidney, "Primitive Monotheism," in *Culture in History: Essays in Honor of Paul Radin*, ed. Stanley Diamond (New York: Columbia University Press, 1960) 363-79. Quoting Radin's 1954 Preface: "'On the whole,' he states, 'I feel that pure monotheism in the late Hebraic, Christian and Mohammedan sense of the term is rare. It is clearly encountered in certain parts of Africa, especially West Africa, and in Polynesia. Its occurrence in aboriginal America and Australia, it seems to me, is more than doubtful. As an essentially philosophic belief entertained by a few deeply religious individuals and connected with origin myths it may, however, appear everywhere.'" In the 1951 publication Radin still regarded the Pawnee as perhaps an example of American primitive monotheism, but even this one exception is not granted in the later publication. "What passes for monotheism in the reports of priests and missionaries is usually some form of monolatry or henotheism" (372). To begin to get at the complexity of Indian thought may require acknowledging that Western categories do not work for identifying, describing, naming, or explaining Indian religious realities.

14. Francis LaFlesche, *A Dictionary of the Osage Language*, Bureau of American Ethnology, Bulletin 109 (Smithsonian, 1932; republished by Indian Tribal Series, 1975).

15. Eugene Buechel, S.J., compiler, and Paul Manhart, S.J., editor, *A Dictionary: Oie Wowapi Wan of Teton Sioux* (Pine Ridge, SD: Red Cloud Indian School, 1970, 1983) 526 and 707.

16. See, for example, Wallace L. Chafe, *Seneca Thanksgiving Rituals*, Bureau of American Ethnology, Bulletin 193 (1961).

17. *Dictionary of the Osage Language*, 193.

18. Dorsey, "Siouan Sociology," 205-44.

19. LaFlesche, "Rite of the Chiefs," 147-50, 357-58.

20. *Dictionary of the Osage Language*, 193.

21. Francis LaFlesche, *The Osage and the Invisible World*, Garrick A. Bailey, ed. (Norman, OK: University of Oklahoma Press, 1995) 31.

22. *The Sun Dance and Other Ceremonies of the Oglala Division of the Teton Sioux*, Anthropological Papers of the American Museum of Natural History, Vol. XVI, Part II (New York: Museum Trustees, 1917). See also the other publications of Walker's papers, especially: Raymond J. De Mallie and Elaine

A. Jahner, eds., *Lakota Belief and Ritual* (Lincoln, NE: University of Nebraska Press, 1980); and Elaine Jahner, ed., *Lakota Myth* (Lincoln, NE: University of Nebraska Press, 1983).

23. In DeMallie and Jahner, *Lakota Belief and Ritual*, 70.

24. Ibid., 95. Walker details this schema of 16 in *The Sun Dance*, 95; see William K. Powers for a recent discussion of this aspect of Walker's interpretation: *Sacred Language: The Nature of Supernatural Discourse in Lakota* (Norman, OK: University of Oklahoma Press, 1986) 122-3.

25. DeMallie and Jahner, *Lakota Belief*, 104.

26. Ibid., 107: "When a child disappeared, Maka (the Earth) was invoked to help return them."

27. Ibid., 35. Compare the comment of Thomas Tyon, who identifies Maka as: "A Presiding Spirit of the Earth which hears invocations and is pleased or displeased and shows this by giving good or bad seasons and by producing plenty or scanty vegetation. This spirit especially presides over the medicines that come from the earth and gives to them potencies for good or evil according to its pleasure and according to the familiarity of the shaman or medicine man with it and the methods of his invocations."

28. Hultkranz, "The Structure of Theistic Beliefs," 21.

29. Eugene Buechel, *A Grammar of Lakota* (St. Francis, SD: St. Francis Mission, 1939). Only context can determine if a word is singular or plural. Some years ago I broke a private vow not to ask questions during a stay in South Dakota. My intuition was to learn the traditional way, by listening and watching. But at the end of my stay I did ask a medicine man, in whose night ceremony I had participated, which Tunkasila we had prayed to. His quick response was: All of them, of course. Unity and diversity. I think there is a definite insight here.

30. William K. Powers, *Yuwipi: Vision and Experience in Ogala Ritual* (Lincoln, NE: University of Nebraska Press, 1982) 68-75.

4. Christology

1. George E. "Tink" Tinker took primary responsibility for this chapter. It brings together material that he published earlier in two separate essays: "Jesus, Corn Mother, and Conquest: Christology and Colonialism," in *Native American Religious Identity: Unforgotten Gods*, Jace Weaver, ed. (Maryknoll, NY: Orbis, 1998); and "American Indians and Jesus: Towards an EATWOT Christology," *Voices from the Third World* (Fall 1995) 115-134 (a special issue edited by James Cone).

2. This ceremony is persistently and wrongly signified in anthropological and history of religions literature as quintessential evidence for the radical individualism of plains Indian societies.

3. For a description of missionary participation in injustices committed against Indian peoples, see Tinker, *Missionary Conquest: The Gospel and Native American Cultural Genocide* (Minneapolis: Fortress, 1993).

4. The first part of the name occurs also in the name Jonathan (*ya - nathan*), which is actually a similar name to Nathaniel (*nathan - el*). These last

two names have a counterpart in two Greek names, one male and one female: Theodore and Dorothy, both combinations of the words for God (*theos*) and gift (*dor*). In Hebrew, *nathan* means gift, while *ya* and *el* are variant names for God, shortened forms of *yahweh* and *elohim*. All mean "gift of god."

5. Theological Anthropology

1. A. Irving Hallowell, *Culture and Experience* (Philadelphia: University of Pennsylvania Press, 1955) 258-59.

2. J. N. B. Hewitt, "Orenda and a Definition of Religion," *American Anthropologist*, n.s., IV (1902) 33-46; W. J. Hoffman, "The Midewiwin, or 'Grand Medicine Society' of the Ojibwa," *Seventh Annual Report of the Bureau of American Ethnology, 1885-86* (Washington, D.C.: U.S. Government Printing Office, 1891) 143-300; James R. Walker, *Lakota Belief and Ritual*, ed. Raymond J. DeMallie and Elaine A. Jahner (Lincoln, NE: University of Nebraska Press, 1980). The symposium proceedings were published as Raymond D. Fogelson and Richard N. Adams, eds., *The Anthropology of Power: Ethnographic Studies from Asia, Oceania, and the New World* (New York: Academic Press, 1977).

3. Lewis Henry Morgan, *Systems of Consanguinity and Affinity in Human Society* (Lincoln, NE: University of Nebraska Press, 1997).

4. Clark Wissler, *Man and Culture* (New York: Thomas Y. Crowell Company, 1923) 49.

5. Clifford Geertz, *The Interpretation of Cultures* (New York: Basic Books, 1973) 5.

6. Jack Kilpatrick, "Verbs are King on Panther Hill," *Southwest Review* (Autumn, 1961) 372-75.

7. Gladys Reichard, *Navaho Religion: A Study in Symbolism* (Princeton: Princeton University Press, 1950) 314.

8. Clifford Geertz, *Local Knowledge: Further Essays in Interpretive Anthropology* (New York: Basic Books, 1983) 90-91.

9. Robert Lowie, *Primitive Religion* (New York: Liveright Publishing Corp., 1924) v.

10. Anthony F. C. Wallace, *Religion: An Anthropological View* (New York: Random House, 1966) 52-101.

11. Leslie Spier, "The Sun Dance of the Plains Indians: Its Development and Diffusion," *Anthropological Papers of the American Museum of Natural History*, XVI, part VII (1921).

12. Ruth Benedict, *The Concept of the Guardian Spirit in North America*, Memoirs of the American Anthropological Association 29 (Menasha, WI: The American Anthropological Association, 1923); Ruth Benedict, *Patterns of Culture* (Boston: Houghton Mifflin Company, Sentry Edition, 1934).

13. Elsie Clews Parsons, *Pueblo Indian Religion*, 2 vols. (Chicago: University of Chicago Press, 1939).

14. Åke Hultkrantz, *Conceptions of the Soul among North American Indians: A Study in Religious Ethnology* (Stockholm: Caslon Press, 1953) 243.

15. Mary Bartholomew Black, "Ojibwa Power Belief System," in *The Anthropology of Power: Ethnographic Studies from Asia; Oceania, and the New World*, ed. Raymond D. Fogelson and Richard N. Adams (New York: Academic Press, 1977); Hope L. Isaacs, *Orenda: An Ethnographic Cognitive Study of Seneca Medicine and Politics* (Unpublished Ph.D. Dissertation, State University of New York at Buffalo, 1973).

16. A. Irving Hallowell, "Ojibwa Ontology, Behavior, and World View," in *Contributions to Anthropology: Selected Papers of A. Irving Hallowell* (Chicago: University of Chicago Press, 1976) 362.

17. Mary Becker Druke, "The Concept of Personhood in Seventeenth and Eighteenth Century Iroquois Ethnopersonality," *Studies in Iroquoian Culture*, ed. Nancy Bonvillain, Occasional Papers I Northeastern Anthropology, no. 6 (George's Mill, NH: Man in the Northeast, Inc., 1980) 60.

18. W. J. Hoffman, "The Midewiwin, or 'Grand Medicine Society' of the Ojibwa," *Seventh Annual Report of the Bureau of Ethnology, 1885-86* (Washington, D.C.: U.S. Government Printing Office, 1891) 168.

19. Gerardus van der Leeuw, *Religion in Essence and Manifestation* (Gloucester, MA: Peter Smith, 1967) 28.

20. Michel Foucault, *The Archaeology of Knowledge and the Discourse on Language*, trans. A. M. Sheridan Smith (New York: Pantheon Books, 1971).

21. Mircea Eliade, *Shamanism: Archaic Techniques of Ecstasy*, trans. Willard R. Trask (Princeton: Princeton University Press, Bollingen Series, LXXVI, 1964) 32.

22. Washington Matthews, *The Night Chant: A Navaho Ceremony* (Salt Lake City: University of Utah Press, 1995) xxvi-xxvii.

23. Hallowell, "Ojibwa Ontology," 377.

24. Claude Lévi-Strauss, *Structural Anthropology*, trans. Claire Jacobson and Brooke Grundfest Schoepf (New York: Basic Books, Inc., 1963).

25. Louis A. Hieb, "Meaning and Mismeaning: Toward an Understanding of the Ritual Clown," in *New Perspectives on the Pueblos*, ed. Alfonso Ortiz (Albuquerque, NM: University of New Mexico Press, 1972) 163-96.

26. Don Talayesva, *Sun Chief: The Autobiography of a Hopi Indian*, ed. Leo Simmons (New Haven, CT: Yale University Press, 1942) 188-89.

27. *Black Elk Speaks: Being the Life Story of a Holy Man of the Oglala Sioux*, as told through John G. Neihardt (Lincoln, NE: University of Nebraska Press, 1961) 192-93.

28. Barbara Tedlock, "The Clown's Way," in *Teachings from the American Earth*, ed. Dennis and Barbara Tedlock (New York: Liveright, 1975) 105-18.

29. Arthur C. Parker, *Seneca Myths and Folk Tales* (Buffalo Historical Society Publications 27, 1923) 59-73.

30. *Black Elk Speaks*, 3-4.

31. Johannes Fabian, *Time and the Other: How Anthropology Makes Its Object* (New York: Columbia University Press, 1983) 25-35.

32. Benjamin Whorf, "An American Indian Model of the Universe," in *Language, Thought, and Reality* (Cambridge, MA: Massachusetts Institute of Technology Press, 1970).

33. Nancy M. Farriss, "Remembering the Future, Anticipating the Past: History, Time, and Cosmology among the Maya of Yucatan," *Journal for Comparative Study of Society and History*, 1987 (29 no. 3) 577.

34. Robert E. Bieder, *Science Encounters the Indian, 1820-1880: The Early Years of American Ethnology* (Norman, OK and London: University of Oklahoma Press, 1986) 60-67.

35. Robert Redfield, Ralph Linton, and Melville J. Herskovits, "A Memorandum on the Study of Acculturation," *American Anthropologist*, XXXVIII, 149-52.

36. Anthony F. C. Wallace, *The Death and Rebirth of the Seneca* (New York: Random House, 1969).

37. Alfred A. Cave, "The Delaware Prophet Neolin: A Reappraisal," *Ethnohistory* 46:2 (Spring 1999) 266-90.

38. James Mooney, *The Ghost-Dance Religion and the Sioux Outbreak of 1890* (Chicago: University of Chicago Press, 1965 [1896]).

39. Clement W. Meighan and Francis A. Riddle, *The Maru Cult of the Pomo Indians: A California Ghost Dance Survival* (Los Angeles, CA: Southwest Museum Press, 1972).

40. Alfonso Ortiz, Lecture to NEH Summer Institute for College Teachers, Newberry Library, Chicago, IL, June 1990.

41. Edward H. Spicer, *Cycles of Conquest: The Impact of Spain, Mexico, and the United States on the Indians of the Southwest, 1533-1960* (Tucson: University of Arizona Press, 1962).

42. Mariasusai Dhavamony, "The Christian Theology of Inculturation," in *Inculturation: Gospel and Culture* (Roma: Editrice Pontificia Universit Gregoriana, 1995).

43. Frank B. Linderman, *Plenty-Coups: Chief of the Crows* (New York: John Day Company, 1957).

44. Douglas Cole, *Captured Heritage: The Scramble for Northwest Coast Artifacts* (Seattle: University of Washington Press, 1985) 122-27.

45. Alice Fletcher and Francis LaFlesche, *The Omaha Tribe*, Twenty-seventh Annual Report of the Bureau of American Ethnology to the Secretary of the Smithsonian Institution, 1905-1906 (Washington, D.C.: U.S. Government Printing Office, 1911).

46. Vine Deloria, Jr., *Custer Died for Your Sins* (New York: Avon Books, 1969) 83.

6. Sin and Ethics

1. Journal of Elliot Mission, April 18, 1821, Papers of the American Board of Commissioners of Foreign Missions, vol. 1, folder 3, Houghton Library, Harvard University.

2. John Ladd, *The Structure of a Moral Code* (Cambridge: Harvard University Press, 1957) 272.

3. Elaine Pagels, *The Gnostic Gospels* (New York: Random House, 1979) 123.

4. Cyrus Byington, *A Dictionary of the Choctaw Language*, eds. J. R.

190   *A Native American Theology*

Swanton, and H. S. Halbert, The Smithsonian Institution, Bureau of American Ethnography, Bulletin 46 (Washington, D.C.: U.S. Government Printing Office, 1915) 375.

5. Henry Willis, personal communication, Norman, OK, Fall, 1997.

6. Roy Harvey Pearce, *Savagism and Civilization* (Baltimore, MD: Johns Hopkins University Press, 1953) 3-24.

7. Benjamin Whorf, "An American Indian Model of the Universe," in *Language, Thought, and Reality*, ed. John B. Carroll (Cambridge, MA: The M.I.T. Press, 1956) 57-64; Frank G. Speck and Leonard Broom, *Cherokee Dance and Drama*, (Norman, OK: University of Oklahoma Press, 1983) 45-53.

8. Frances Densmore, "Uses of Plants by the Chippewa Indians," *Forty-fourth Annual Report of the Bureau of American Ethnology, 1926-27* (Washington, D.C.: U.S. Government Printing Office, 1928; 5-397) 285-397.

9. *Black Elk Speaks: Being the Life Story of a Holy Man of the Oglala Sioux*, as told through John G. Neihardt (Lincoln, NE: University of Nebraska Press, 1961) 67-72.

10. Ruth Landes, *Ojibwa Religion and the Midewiwin* (Madison: University of Wisconsin Press, 1968) 42-43.

11. See, for instance, the account of the killing of a woman suspected of witchcraft among the Choctaw Indians in Mississippi. H. B. Cushman, *History of the Choctaw, Chickasaw and Natchez Indians*, ed. Angie Debo (Norman, OK: University of Oklahoma Press, 1999) 74-75.

12. Elaine Pagels, *Adam, Eve and the Serpent* (New York: Vintage Books, 1989) 27.

13. James R. Walker, *Lakota Belief and Ritual*, ed. Raymond J. DeMallie and Elaine A. Jahner (Lincoln, NE: University of Nebraska Press, 1980) 28.

14. Peter J. Powell, *Sweet Medicine* (Norman, OK: University of Oklahoma Press, 1969) II, 446; Karl N. Llewelyn and E. Adamson Hobel, *The Cheyenne Way* (Norman, OK: University of Oklahoma Press, 1941) 187, 203-204; John C. Ewers, *The Blackfeet: Raiders on the Northwestern Plains* (Norman, OK: University of Oklaoma Press, 1958) 98.

15. James C. Adair, *History of the The American Indians*, ed. Samuel Cole Williams (New York: Promontory Press, 1930) 146.

16. Ernestine Friedl, *Women and Men: An Anthropologist's View* (Prospect Heights, IL: Waveland Press, 1975).

17. Karl Luckert, *The Navajo Hunter Tradition* (Tucson: University of Arizona Press, 1975) 62.

18. *Sun Chief: The Autobiography of a Hopi Indian*, ed. Leo Simmons (New Haven, CT: Yale University Press, 1942) 181.

19. Berard Haile, *Women Versus Men: A Conflict of Navajo Emergence* (Lincoln, NE: University of Nebraska Press, 1981) 9-35.

20. John Swanton, *Source Material for the Social and Ceremonial Life of the Choctaw Indians*, Smithsonian Institution, Bureau of American Ethnology Bulletin 103 (Washington, D.C.: U.S. Government Printing Office, 1931) 218.

21. Alfonso Ortiz, *The Tewa World: Space, Time, Being and Becoming in a*

Pueblo Society (Chicago: University of Chicago Press, 1969) 50.

22. Leland C.Wyman, *The Mountainway of the Navajo* (Tucson: University of Arizona Press, 1975) 136-42.

23. James Mooney, *Myths of the Cherokee and Sacred Formulas of the Cherokees*, reprinted from 19th (1900) and 7th (1891) Annual Reports of the Bureau of American Ethnology (Nashville, TN: Charles and Randy Elder, 1982) 239.

24. Paul G. Zolbrod, *Diné behané': The Navajo Creation Story* (Albuquerque, NM: University of New Mexico Press, 1984) 1-89.

25. Stephen C. McCluskey, "Historical Archaeoastronomy: The Hopi Example," in *Archaeoastronomy in the New World: American Primitive Astronomy*, ed. A. F. Aveni (Cambridge: Cambridge Univ. Press, 1982).

26. Gary Witherspoon, *Language and Art in the Navajo Universe* (Ann Arbor: University of Michigan Press, 1977) 25.

27. A. Irving Hallowell, "Ojibwa Ontology, Behavior, and World View," in *Contributions to Anthropology: Selected Papers of A. Irving Hallowell* (Chicago, IL: University of Chicago Press, 1976) 383-84.

28. Richard B. Brandt, *Hopi Ethics: A Theoretical Analysis* (Chicago: University of Chicago Press, 1954, reprinted 1974) 39-40.

29. Ibid., 42.

30. Ladd, 272.

31. Knud Rasmussen, *The Intellectual Culture of Iglulik Eskimos*, trans. William Worster (Copenhagen: Report of the 5th Thule Expedition, Vol. 7, no. 1, 1929) 55-56.

32. *William Bartram on the Southeastern Indians*, ed. and annotated by Gregory A. Waselkov and Kathryn E. Holland Braund (Lincoln, NE: University of Nebraska Press, 1995) 124-25.

33. Keith Basso, *Wisdom Sits in Places: Landscape and Language Among the Western Apache* (Albuquerque: University of New Mexico Press, 1996) 56-57.

34. James Axtell, *The Invasion Within: The Contest of Cultures in Colonial North America* (New York and Oxford: Oxford University Press, 1985) 135.

35. H. B. Cushman, *History of the Choctaw, Chickasaw and Natchez Indians*, ed. Angie Debo (New York: Russell & Russell, 1962) 101-102.

7. Trickster

1. Jace Weaver took primary responsibility for this chapter.

2. Jace Weaver, "From I-Hermeneutics to We-Hermeneutics: Native Americans and the Post-Colonial," in *Native American Religious Identity: Unforgotten Gods* (Maryknoll, NY: Orbis Books, 1998) 19.

3. Lewis Hyde, *Trickster Makes This World: Mischief, Myth, and Art* (New York: Farrar, Straus and Giroux, 1998) 6.

4. James De Sauza and Harriet Rohmer, *Brother Anansi and the Cattle Ranch* (San Francisco: Children's Book Press, 1989) 5.

5. Jack F. and Anna Kilpatrick, *Friends of Thunder: Folktales of the Oklahoma Cherokee* (Dallas, TX: Southern Methodist University Press, 1964) 99.

6. Richard Erdoes and Alfonso Ortiz, eds. *American Indian Trickster Tales* (New York: Viking, 1998) xvi.

7. Ibid., xviii.

8. Hyde, 130.

9. Erdoes and Ortiz, xviii.

10. Hyde, 9. Emphasis mine.

11. Quoted in Erdoes and Ortiz., xix.

12. Hyde, 9.

13. Ibid., 13.

14. Ibid., 10.

15. Paul Radin, *The Trickster* (New York: Schocken Books, 1972) xxiii.

16. Hyde, 10-11.

17. See generally, Homer Noley, *First White Frost* (Nashville: Abingdon Books, 1991).

18. See, Gerald Vizenor, *Manifest Manners: Postindian Warriors of Survivance* (Hanover: Wesleyan University Press, 1994) 122; Louis Owens, "'Ecstatic Strategies': Gerald Vizenor's *Darkness in Saint Louis Bearheart*," in *Narrative Chance: Postmodern Discourse on Native American Indian Literatures*, ed. Gerald Vizenor (Norman, OK: University of Oklahoma Press, 1993) 141-53.

19. Hyde, 12.

20. Alan Velie, "The Trickster Novel," in *Narrative Chance*, 136.

21. Hyde, 9-10.

22. Sister Charles Palm, *Stories Jesus Told: Dakota Way of Life* (Sioux Falls, SD: American Indian Research Center, Blue Cloud Abbey, 1985) 50-58. For an account of the life of Sweet Medicine, see, Peter J. Powell, *Sweet Medicine* (Norman, OK: University of Oklahoma Press, 1969), vol. 2, 460-66. See also, Jace Weaver, "Native Americans and Religious Education," in *Multicultural Religious Education*, ed. Barbara Wilkerson (Birmingham, AL: Religious Education Press, 1997) 282.

23. Quoted in Erdoes and Ortiz, xxi.

8. Land

1. Dan Georgakas, *The Broken Hoop* (New York: Zenith Books, 1973) 3.

2. Oswald Werner and Kenneth Y. Begishe, *The Anatomical Atlas of the Navajo* (Evanston, IL: Northwestern University, 1966).

3. Lynn Cesi, "Fish Fertilizer: A Native North American Practice?" *Science*, 1975, 188: 26-30.

4. Edward Nequatewa, *Truth of a Hopi* (Flagstaff, AZ: Museum of Northern Arizona, 1967); Paul Zolbrod, *Diné bahane': The Navajo Creation Story* (Albuquerque, NM: University of New Mexico Press, 1984).

5. James R. Murie, *Ceremonies of the Pawnee*, ed. Douglas R. Parks (Lincoln, NE: University of Nebraska Press, 1981).

6. Arthur C. Parker, *Seneca Myths and Folk Tales*, Buffalo Historical Society Publications 27 (1923) 59-73.

7. Dan Georgakas, *Red Shadows* (New York: Zenith Books, 1973) 15.

8. John Opie, "Frontier History in Environmental Perspective," in *The American West: New Perspectives, New Dimensions*, ed. Jerome O. Steffen (Norman, OK: University of Oklahoma Press, 1979) 17-18.

9. John Opie, *Nature's Nation: An Environmental History of the United States* (Fort Worth, TX: Harcourt Brace College Publishers, 1998).

10. Paul W. Gates, *The Jeffersonian Dream: Studies in the History of American Land Policy and Development*, ed. Allan G. and Margaret Beattie Bogue (Albuquerque, NM: University of New Mexico Press, 1996); Vernon Carstensen, ed., *The Public Lands: Studies in the History of the Public Domain* (Madison, WI: University of Wisconsin Press, 1968); William Cronon, *Changes in the Land: Indians, Colonists, and the Ecology of New England* (New York: Hill and Wang, 1983).

11. Reginald Horsman, *Expansion and American Indian Policy, 1782-1812* (Norman: University of Oklahoma Press, [1992], 1967) 126-50; see also Wilbur Jacobs, *Dispossessing the American Indian: Indians and Whites on the Colonial Frontier* (New York: [n.p.] 1972). Jacobs compares the colonialism to European and indigenous experiences in Australia and New Guinea.

12. *Johnson v. McIntosh*, 21 U.S. (Wheat.) 543, 5 L. Ed. 681 (1823).

13. Claire Farrar, *Living Life's Circle: Mescalero Apache Cosmovision* (Albuquerque, NM: University of New Mexico Press, 1991) 140-83.

14. *Caldwell v. The State of Alabama*, 1 Stew. and Potter (Ala.) 327 (1832); Vine Deloria, Jr., ed., *Of Utmost Good Faith* (New York: Bantam Books, 1972) 11.

15. Ibid., 12.

16. Ibid.

17. Ibid., 42-43.

18. Ibid.

19. Richard Henry Pratt, *Battlefield and Classroom: Four Decades with the American Indian, 1867-1904* (Lincoln, NE: University of Nebraska Press, 1964) 266.

20. Wilcomb Washburn, *The Assault on Indian Tribalism: The General Allotment Law (Dawes Act) of 1887* (Philadelphia: Lippincott, 1975).

21. David Wallace Adams, *Education for Extinction: American Indians and the Boarding School Experience, 1875-1928* (Lawrence, KS: University Press of Kansas, 1995) 52.

22. Deloria, *Of Utmost Good Faith*, 264.

23. Ibid., 261.

24. Ibid.

25. Ibid., 269.

26. Winona LaDuke, "Recovering the Land," *Blueprint for Social Action*, (Vol. LI, no. 5) 1-98.

27. Quoted in William T. Hagan, *Theodore Roosevelt and Six Friends of the Indian* (Norman, OK: University of Oklahoma Press, 1997) 79.

28. Ronald Goodman, *Lakota Star Knowledge* (Rosebud, SD: Sintje Gleske College, 1992) 11-14.

29. James C. Olson, *Red Cloud and the Sioux Problem* (Lincoln, NE: University of Nebraska Press, 1965) 58-82.

30. Roxanne Dunbar Ortiz, *The Great Sioux Nation* (New York: American Indian Treaty Council; Berkeley: Moon Books, 1977) 25.

31. Edward Lazarus, *Black Hills/White Justice: The Sioux Nation Versus the United States: 1775 to the Present* (New York: HarperCollins, 1991) 375-76.

32. Alexandra New Holy, "The Heart of Everything That Is: Paha Sapa, Treaties, and Lakota Identity" *Oklahoma City University Law Review*, 23, nos. 1 and 2 (1998) 317-52.

33. LaDuke, 6

34. LaDuke, 4.

35. LaDuke, 2.

36. Georgakas, *Red Shadows*; see Crisca Bierwert, "Remembering Chief Seattle: Reversing Cultural Studies of a Vanishing Native American," *American Indian Quarterly*, 22, no. 3 (Summer 1998) 280-304.

9. Eschatology

1. Jace Weaver took primary responsibility for this chapter.

2. Paul Tillich, *Shaking the Foundations* (New York: Charles Scribner's Sons, 1948) 141-42.

3. E. Stanley Jones, *The Christ of the Indian Road* (New York: Abingdon Press, 1925) 5.

4. Jace Weaver, *That the People Might Live: Native American Literatures and Native American Community* (New York: Oxford University Press, 1997) 182.

5. Leslie D. Weatherhead, *The Christian Agnostic* (Nashville: Abingdon Books, 1965) 295-96.

6. Ibid., 293-97.

7. Jace Weaver, *American Journey: The Native American Experience*. Book on CD-ROM, key topic essay "The End of the World" (Woodbridge, CT: Research Publications, 1999).

8. Ibid.

9. Ibid.

10. Ibid.

11. Deloria, *God Is Red: A Native View of Religion* (Golden, CO: Fulcrum, 1992) 195.

12. Weaver, *American Journey*.

13. Ibid.

14. James Mooney, *History, Myths, and Sacred Formulas of the Cherokees*, reprint (Asheville, NC: Historical Images, 1992) 335-36.

15. William G. McLoughlin, *Cherokee Renascence in the New Republic* (Princeton: Princeton University Press, 1986) 184-85.

16. Jorge Noriega, "The Shadows of Power: An Ethnographic Account of Apache Shamanism" (unpublished paper, 1994) 40-41, 43.

17. Ibid., 41.

18. Thomas R. Henry, *Wilderness Messiah* (New York: Bonanza Books, 1955) 148.

19. James Mooney, *The Ghost Dance Religion and the Sioux Outbreak of*

1890, no. 14, pt. 2 (Washington: Bureau of American Ethnology, 1896) 749-56; Vittorio Lanternari, *The Religions of the Oppressed: A Study of Modern Messianic Cults* (New York: Alfred A. Knopf, 1963) 124-28.

20. Noriega, 42-43.

21. Ibid., 43.

22. Ibid.

23. Paul Steinmetz, *Meditations with Native Americans: Lakota Spirituality* (Santa Fe, NM: Bear & Company,1984) 15-16.

24. Elizabeth Cook-Lynn, "A Monograph of a Peyote Singer: Asa Primeaux, Sr.," *Wicazo Sa Review* (Spring 1991) 2.

25. Emerson Spider, Sr., "The Native American Church of Jesus Christ," in *Sioux Indian Religion*, ed. DeMallie and Parks (Norman, OK: University of Oklahoma Press, 1987) 189-209.

26. Cook-Lynn, 10-15.

27. Vincent Catches, "Native American Church: The Half-Moon Way," *Wicazo Sa Review* (Spring 1991) 17-23.

28. Aiban Wagua, "Station VI: Jesus Is Scourged and Crowned with Thorns," in Virgil Elizondo, ed., *Way of the Cross: The Passion of Christ in the Americas* (Maryknoll, NY: Orbis Books, 1992) 48.

29. Jack D. Forbes, *Columbus and Other Cannibals* (Brooklyn: Autonomedia, 1992) 128.

30. Elsa Tamez, "Reliving Our Histories: Racial and Cultural Revelations of God," in David Batstone, ed., *New Visions for the Americas: Religious Engagement and Social Transformation* (Minneapolis: Fortress Press, 1993) 33ff.

31. Robert Boissiere, *The Return of Pahana* (Santa Fe, NM: Bear & Company, 1990) 70.

32. Baldridge, "Christianity," 9; "Reclaiming," 29.

33. Deloria, *God*, 185-87.

34. William Apess, "The Indians: The Ten Lost Tribes," in *On Our Own Ground: The Complete Writings of William Apess, a Pequot*, ed. Barry O'Connell (Amherst, MA: University of Massachusetts Press, 1992) 114.

35. Weaver, *That the People Might Live*, 182.

36. Jace Weaver, "Messianism in Native American Spiritual Concepts: Or, "Who Do We Say He Is—Discerning the Christ of the Red Road" (Unpublished paper) 11-12.

37. Diane Glancy, "Two Dresses," in *I Tell You Now*, ed. Brian Swann and Arnold Krupat (Lincoln, NE: University of Nebraska Press, 1987) 174.

38. Jace Weaver, "Interpreting a Vision of a Red Bear," *Native Journal* (August 1992) 4.

39. Gerald Vizenor, "The Baron of Patronia," in *Talking Leaves*, ed. Craig Lesley (New York: Laurel, 1991) 286-87.

40. Wagua, 48.

41. Gustavo Gutiérrez, "Only My Death Can Express My Life," in Elizondo, 9.

42. John Macquarrie, *Paths in Spirituality* (New York: Harper & Row, 1972) 112.

43. For an African perspective, see also, F. Eboussi Boulaga, *Christianity*

without Fetishes: An African Critique and Recapture of Theology (Maryknoll, NY: Orbis Books, 1984).

Afterword

1. E. Donald Two-Rivers, *Survivor's Medicine* (Norman, OK: University of Oklahoma Press, 1998) 205.

2. Robert Allen Warrior, *Tribal Secrets: Recovering American Indian Intellectual Traditions* (Minneapolis, MN: University of Minnesota Press, 1995) 126.

INDEX

accommodation, 97

acculturation, 8, 96-97, 177

Adam and Eve, 35, 86, 101-102

Aiban Wagua, 162, 164

Algonquian, 90

American Board of Commissioners for Foreign Missions, 101

American Indian Religious Freedom Act, 175

Anansi, 114-115, 123

ancestors, 48, 52, 71, 75, 82, 97, 129, 147, 174

anthropology, 85-87, 91, 96, 98-99, 166

Apache: Chirachua, 154; Cibecue, 18, 111, 157-158; Mescalero, 134; Silas John, 159

Apess, William, 5, 163

Aristotle, 39; Aristotelean logic, 87

Ashanti, 115

atonement, 163, 165

Aua, 110

Augustine, 103, 151

Axtell, James, 7

Aztec, 153

Bad Wound, 60

balance, the concept of, 18, 32-36, 40-48, 51, 107-112, 117, 148

balancing cultural values and Christianity, 11, 23, 65-68

baptism, 113, 161

beginnings, 34-38

Benedict, Ruth, 88

benevolent institutions, 7

Berkhofer, Robert, 132

Bible, 2, 21-23, 48-50, 70-78, 141-143, 158-161

bi-gender, God as, 17, 79

bigotry, 136, 177

Black Elk, 92, 102, 160

Blackfeet, 37, 117

Black God, 108

Black Hills, 140, 170

Black Kettle, 176

Blackmun, Justice Harry, 175

boarding schools, 8, 30

Boas, Franz, 92, 99

Boff, Leonardo, 113

Bogachiddy, 108

Bola Maru, 97

Brer Rabbit, 124

Buddhists, 151

Bureau of Indian Affairs, 177

Byington, Cyrus, 19, 101

California, 97, 116, 154

Canada, 16, 79, 89, 173

Carlisle Indian School, 137

casino gaming, 179

Catches, Vincent, 161

Catholicism: Church, 9; original sin, 19; rituals, 9; saints, 9; sin of pride, 6, 111

197